For Lou Nanni —
With my gratitude and
best wishes always to you
and Carmen —

Samuel Hazo
7/4/2014

And the Time Is

Other Works by Samuel Hazo

Poetry

Sexes: The Marriage Dialogues
Like a Man Gone Mad
The Song of the Horse
A Flight to Elsewhere
Just Once
As They Sail
The Holy Surprise of Right Now
The Past Won't Stay behind You
Silence Spoken Here
Nightwords
The Color of Reluctance

Thank a Bored Angel
To Paris
Quartered
Once for the Last Bandit
Twelve Poems
Blood Rights
My Sons in God
Listen with the Eye
The Quiet Wars
Discovery

Fiction

The Time Remaining
This Part of the World
Stills

The Wanton Summer Air
The Very Fall of the Sun
Inscripts

Criticism

*Smithereened Apart: A Critique of
    Hart Crane*

Essays

The Stroke of a Pen
The Power of Less
*The Pittsburgh That Stays within
    You*

The Feast of Icarus
The Rest Is Prose
Spying for God
The Autobiographers of Everybody

Plays

Watching Fire, Watching Rain
*Mano A Mano: A Flamenco Drama
    (The Life of Manolete)*
Feather
Solos
Until I'm Not Here Anymore

And the Time Is

POEMS, 1958–2013

Samuel Hazo

Syracuse University Press

First Edition 2014

14 15 16 17 18 19   6 5 4 3 2 1

"No Echo in Judea," "Postscript to Many Letters," "Preface to a Poetry Reading," "To a Commencement of Scoundrels" by Samuel Hazo, from *Thank a Bored Angel*, copyright ©1983 by Samuel Hazo. Reprinted by permission of New Directions Publishing Corp. "A City Made Sacred Because Your Son's Grandfather Died in It," "Only the New Branches Bloom," "The Next Time You Were There," "The Toys," "Maps for a Song are Drawn as You Go," "The Bearing," "The Silence at the Bottom of the Well," "Waiting for Zero" by Samuel Hazo, from *To Paris*, copyright ©1974, 1976, 1977, 1978, 1980, 1981 by Samuel Hazo. Reprinted by permission of New Directions Publishing Corp.

∞ The paper used in this publication meets the minimum requirements of the American National Standard for Information Sciences—Permanence of Paper for Printed Library Materials, ANSI Z39.48-1992.

For a listing of books published and distributed by Syracuse University Press, visit www.Syracuse UniversityPress.syr.edu.

ISBN: 978-0-8156-1017-5 (cloth)   978-0-8156-5216-8 (e-book)

Library of Congress Cataloging-in-Publication Data
Hazo, Samuel, 1928– author.
   [Poems. Selections]
   And the time is : poems, 1958–2013 / Samuel Hazo. — First edition.
      pages cm
   ISBN 978-0-8156-1017-5 (cloth : alk. paper) — ISBN 978-0-8156-5216-8 (ebook)
   I. Title.
   PS3515.A9877A6 2014
   811'.54—dc23   2014012835

Manufactured in the United States of America

For Samuel Robert Hazo

And yet what is the present
　　but a future that the past
　　made possible?

　　　　—From "Home Are the Sailors"

THE AUTHOR of more than thirty books of poetry, fiction, essays, and plays, Samuel Hazo is the founder and director of the International Poetry Forum in Pittsburgh, Pennsylvania. He is also McAnulty Distinguished Professor of English, Emeritus, at Duquesne University. From 1950 to 1957 he served in the United States Marine Corps, completing his tour as a captain. He graduated magna cum laude from the University of Notre Dame, and received his master's degree from Duquesne University and his doctorate from the University of Pittsburgh. Some of his most recent books are *Like a Man Gone Mad* and *The Song of the Horse* (poetry), *The Time Remaining* and *This Part of the World* (Fiction), *The Stroke of a Pen* and *The Power of Less* (essays), and *Watching Fire, Watching Rain* (drama). He has also translated essays by Denis de Rougemont and the poems of Adonis and Nadia Tueni. His book of poems, *Just Once: New and Previous Poems*, received the Maurice English Poetry Award in 2003. The University of Notre Dame, from which he received the Griffin Award for Creative Writing in 2005, awarded him the tenth of his twelve honorary doctorates in 2008. A National Book Award finalist, he was chosen the first State Poet of the Commonwealth of Pennsylvania by Governor Robert Casey in 1993, and he served until 2003.

Contents

Contents

Contents

Contents

Contents

Preface

Choosing poems to be included in an omnibus volume of one's work over a fifty-five-year period is not a minor challenge. Which poems should be included? Which ones should not be, and why?

Some authors have simplified the matter by including all their work and letting the readers and critics do the evaluating. Still others have used the occasion as a time to let their personal preferences have the last word.

I have chosen the second option. My reasons are that there were poems of mine that I thought were fine when I wrote them, but that feeling ebbed over time. On the other hand, there were others that seemed and still seem as present to me as they were when I wrote them. I have included these poems as the ones I would like to be judged by.

The order is more or less chronological except in several instances where I have paired or grouped poems which, though written at different times, are linked by subject matter or theme.

I would like to express my appreciation to Jo McDougall for a number of thoughtful and perceptive suggestions vis-à-vis some of the more recent poems. Finally, I want to give public thanks and credit to the late Thomas J. Donnelly for his longstanding support of several projects of mine whose primary purpose was to enhance the place of poetry in public speech.

As always, I would like to express my gratitude to my dearest Mary Anne for her patience over the years when I was preoccupied with the writing of a poem and wondering where it was leading me.

Acknowledgments

Grateful acknowledgment is made to the editors and publishers of the following journals, magazines, or books: *American Scholar, Antaeus, Antioch Review, Arts and Letters Daily, Atlantic Monthly, Beloit Poetry Journal, Carolina Quarterly, Cedar Rock, Chicago Choice, Commonweal, The Critic, Crosscurrents, Dickinson Review, Four Quarters, Georgia Review, Greenfield Review, Harper's Magazine, Hawai'i Pacific Review, Hollins Critic, Hopkins Review, Hudson Review, Image, Janus Head, Kansas City Review, Kenyon Review, Malahat Review, Mediterranean Review, Mid-Century American Poetry Review, Michigan Quarterly Review, minnesota review* [sic], *Mississippi Review, Mystique, New Directions in Prose and Poetry 41, New Letters, New Orleans Review, New York Times, Notre Dame Review, Notre Dame Magazine, Ontario Review, Organica, Painted Bird, Pittsburgh Post-Gazette, Poetry Miscellany, Prairie Schooner, Sagatrieb, Salmagundi, Samizdat, Saturday Review, September 11, 2001: American Writers Respond, Sewanee Review, Shenandoah, Southern Review, Stand, Tar River Poetry, Texas Observer, Texas Quarterly, Transatlantic Review, Virginia Quarterly, Review, Water*Stone, Worcester Review,* and *Yale Review.*

Special thanks to the University of Arkansas Press for permission to reprint poems that first appeared in *The Past Won't Stay Behind You, The Holy Surprise Of Right Now,* and *As They Sail,* and to Autumn House Press for permission to reprint poems from *The Song of the Horse.*

The first section of the "At the Site of the Memorial" is engraved at the entrance to the park in Harrisburg, Pennsylvania, that honors those Pennsylvanians awarded the Congressional Medal of Honor from the Civil War to the present, as well as on the Herstead Memorial for the fallen from all the services in Scottsbluff, Nebraska.

"Home Are the Sailors" is the text of a symphonic composition by my son, Samuel Robert Hazo. It had its world premiere in New York on May 11, 2011, at Carnegie Hall, by the Notre Dame Band.

"Towels" and "The Necessary Brevity of Pleasures" were presented by Garrison Keillor on *The Writer's Amanac*.

And the Time Is

Lost Swimmer

Each poem I surprise from hiding
   is a face I learn to draw
   by drawing it.
                  Masterplan?
None.
       Strategy?
                None except
   whatever wits I pit
   against myself to bring it
off.
      Never the face
   imagined nor a face in fact,
   my making is its own solution.
It tells me how *it* must
   become, and I obey or else.
I see myself as some
   lost swimmer of the night
   who must discover where
   he goes by going.
                Uncertain,
   dared and curious, I stall
   my dive until the surface
   stills its saucered ditto
   of the moon.
             Then, plunge...
Sleep's inland waves lock over
   me.
      Ashore, the sealevel
   world of pistols, porkchops,
   mirrors and garbage ripens
   into headlines.
          But where I
   plummet, horses race on wings,

water burns, and willows
write their reasons in the wind.
The pure imagination of a dream
is mine to swim until
the baiting light betrays
me.
      And I rise.
            The shore
steadies where I left it.
                The whole
unfloatable and failing world
goes by as given.
          I swim
from maybe to the merely real
and make them one with words.
I wonder how I did
it.
      I wondered how I'll do
it.
      And I've done it.

PART ONE

Anticipating Yesterday, Remembering Tomorrow

Postscript to Many Letters

While other brothers meet and talk like foes
or strangers or alumni—hostile, cool,
or banal—brotherhood is still our binding.
Somehow we have survived disintegration
since the quiet, Pittsburgh afternoons we walked
in rain bareheaded, scarfless, flaunting health,
the nights we smoked large, academic pipes
and read and talked philosophy, the years
of seminars and uniforms and trips
and letters postmarked Paris, Quantico,
Beirut, Jerusalem and San Francisco.

Nothing has changed or failed, and still we have
"the same heroes and think the same men fools."
Our heroes still are individuals
resolved to face their private absolutes.
We see the fool in all who fail themselves
by choice and turn and all promise cold with talk.
A Levantine who saw such folly done
two thousand years ago grew bored with life
and said only the unborn were worth blessing.
Not sticks, not any, not the sharpest stones
can bruise or break the unbegotten bones.

Yet, fools and our few heroes will persist.
We cannot bless the unborn flesh or wish
our times and cities back to countrysides
when wigwams coned into a twist of poles.
The future holds less answers than the past.
Salvation lies in choice, in attitude,
in faith that mocks glib gospelers who leave
the name of Jesus whitewashed on a cliff.

We still can shun what shames or shams
the day and keep as one our vigor in the bond
of blood where love is fierce but always fond.

Carol of a Father

He runs ahead to ford a flood of leaves—
he suddenly a forager and I
the lagging child content to stay behind
and watch the gold upheavals at the curb
submerge his surging ankles and subside.

A word could leash him back or make him turn
and ask me with his eyes if he should stop.
One word, and he would be a son again
and I a father sentenced to correct
a boy's caprice to shuffle in the drifts.

Ignoring fatherhood, I look away
and let him roam in his Octobering
to mint the memory of those few falls
when a boy can wade the quiet avenues
alone, and the sound of leaves solves everything.

God and Man

After casting the first act, checking sections
of scenery and mastering His rage
because the female lead blundered on page
one, He left the actors to themselves on stage
without a script and fretting for directions.

Preface to a Poetry Reading

Since eyes are deaf, and ears are blind to words
in all their ways, I speak the sounds I write,
hoping you see what somehow stays unheard
and hear what never is quite clear at sight.

Bellbeat

The tongue of the bell must bang
   the bell's cold shell
   aloud to make the bell
   a bell.
         No otherwise exists.
What else is every iron
   peartop but an iron
   peartop if it simply cups
   its centered stamen still?
The frozen pendulum strikes
   nil.
       It plumblines
   down like double hands
   made one at half past six.
I've seen the carilloning
   tulips battened down
   in belfries.
         I've heard them
   rock and creak in rainy
   winds.
       I've felt the dangled
   nubs inch close to sound
   but never close enough
   before the muting night
   enshrines them in their brass
   monotony.
        It takes the tugging
   down and easing up
   on one low-knotted rope
   to jell the shape and sound
   of what remembers to become
   a bell.

And gong after gong
it goes, it goes, it goes . . .
And tones go sheeping over,
after, under one
another, shuddering in high
cascades from quick to quiet.
The muffled bellbeat
in my chest rhymes every
beat of the bell with breath.
It tolls my seven circles
in the sun.

It thunders in my
wrists.

It does not rest.

My Roosevelt Coupé

Coax it, clutch it, kick it
   in the gas was every dawn's
   scenario.
             Then off it bucked,
   backfiring down the block to show
   it minded.
              Each fender gleamed
   a different hue of blue.
Each hubcap chose
   its hill to spin freewheeling
   into traffic.
             I fretted like a spouse
   through chills and overboiling,
   jacked my weekly flats
   and stuffed the spavined seats
   with rags.
             Leaking, the radiator
   healed with swigs of Rinso,
   brake fluid and rainwater.
              Simonized,
   the hood stuck out like a tramp
   in a tux.
           All trips were dares.
Journeys were sagas.
             From Norfolk
   to New York and back,
   I burned eleven quarts
   of oil, seven fuses
   and the horn.
            One headlight
   dimmed with cataracts.
             The other
   funneled me one-eyed

through darker darks than darkness . . .
O my Roosevelt coupé, my first,
my Chevrolet of many scars
and heart attacks, where are you
now?
          Manhandled, you'd refuse
to budge.
          Stick-shifted
into low, you'd enigmatically
reverse.
          Sold finally
for scrap, you waited on your treads
while I pocketed thirty
pieces of unsilver and slunk
away—Wild Buck Hazo
abandoning his first and favorite
mount, unwilling to malinger
long enough to hear
the bullet he could never fire.

The Torch of Blood

Down on my knees and palms
   beside my son, I rediscover
   doormats, rugnaps,
   rockerbows and walljoints
   looming into stratospheres
   of ceiling.
              A telephone
rings us apart.
                I'm plucked
by God's hooks up
from Scylla through an open door,
Charybdis in a socket and a Cyclops
lamp that glares floorlevel
souls away from too much
light to lesser darknesses
What god in what machine
   shall pluck my son?
                 Amid
the Carthage of his toys, he waits
unplucked, unpluckable.
                   I
gulliver my way around
his hands and leave him stalled
before the Matterhorn of one
of seven stairs.
              Floorbound,
he follows, finds and binds
my knees with tendrils of receiver
cord.
        I'm suddenly Laocoon
at bay, condemned to hear
some telephoning Trojan offer

me a more prudential life
where I can wake insured
against disaster, sickness, age
and sundry acts of Genghis
God.
            Meanwhile, I'm slipping
tentacles and watching my
confounding namesake toddle free. . . .
Bloodbeats apart, he shares
    with me the uninsurable air.
We breathe it into odysseys
    where everyone has worlds to cross
    and anything can happen.
Like some blind prophet
    cursed with truth, I wish
    my son his round of stumbles
    to define his rise.
                    Nothing
    but opposites can ground him
    to the lowest heights where men
    go, Lilliputian but redeemable.
Before or after Abraham,
    what is the resurrection and the life
    except a father's word
    remembered in his son?
                    What more
    is Isaac or the Lord?
                    Breath
    and breathgiver are one, and both
    are always now as long
    as flesh remembers.
                    No
    testament but that lives on.
The torch of blood is anyone's

to carry.

        I say so as my son's
father, my father's son.

To a Bicyclist in France

You mail me postcards stamped in Paris—
Notre Dame *illuminée*, the ferried Seine,
the usual best-foot-forward city scenes.
Saying you miss the States, your words are pure

civilian now—all rank and rancor buried
with the notes you typed from BOQ.s another
breed ago. You left the generals
their Jeeps and crew-cuts for a biker's tour

of Europe on your saved-up pay, and shunned
the niche your father wanted you to fit . . .
The ex-lieutenant in me wakes and shakes
me ten years back. I could have biked from Caen,

have cashed my bonds and severance for fare
and pedaled humming through Montmartre, Versailles,
Provence and downward to Marseilles, but I
had someone else to be with somewhere next

to go and with something there to do. My past
leaves Europe still mere names to me. At times
I have regrets—re-plot alternatives
I could have lived—pronounce my lived years lost. . . .

Yet I can write without a hint of cant
I ride with you across the fact of France
as fast as I can think since thinking takes
me where I am despite these accidents

of place. Paris by night and Pittsburgh hills
are similarly still at 4:00 a.m.

Stillness is stillness, life is life, and earth
remains the earth with days quite short, and nights

shorter, and trips the shortest prank of chance.
Apart, we breathe this day alike and stand
an equal distance from eternity—
you there in the U.S.A., me here in France.

For George James

To a Commencement of Scoundrels

My boys, we lied to you.
The world by definition stinks
of Cain, no matter what
your teachers told you. Heroes
and the fools of God may rise
like accidental green
on gray saharas, but the sand
stays smotheringly near.

Deny me if you can. Already
you are turning into personnel,
manpower, figures on a list
of earners, voters, prayers,
soldiers, payers, sums
of population tamed with forms:
last name, middle name, first name—
telephone—date of birth—

home address—age—hobbies—
experience. Tell them the truth.
Your name is Legion. You
are aged a million. Tell
them that. Say you breathe
between appointments: first day,
last day. The rest is no
one's business. Boys, the time

is prime for prophecy.
Books break down their bookends.
Paintings burst their frames.
The world is more than reason's
peanut. Homer sang it real,
Goya painted it, and Shakespeare

staged it for the pelting rinds
of every groundling of the Globe.

Wake up! Tonight the lions
hunt in Kenya. They
can eat a man. Rockets
are spearing through the sky.
They can blast a man to nothing.
Rumor prowl like rebellions.
They can knife a man. No one
survives for long, my boys.

Flesh is always in season:
lusted after, gunned, grenaded,
tabulated through machines,
incinerated, beaten to applause,
anesthetized, autopsied, mourned.
The blood of Troy beats on
in Goya's paintings and the truce
of Lear. Reason yourselves

to that, my buckaroos,
before you rage for God,
country and siss-boom-bah!
You won't, of course. Your schooling
left you trained to serve
like cocksure Paul before
God's lightning smashed
him from his saddle. So—

I wish you what I wish
myself: hard questions
and the nights to answer them,
the grace of disappointment

and the right to seem the fool
for justice. That's enough.
Cowards might ask for more.
Heroes have died for less.

No Echo in Judea

As I drive south to Christ and Abraham,
the tires speed the desert road before
me back to Syria. The clocks have stopped.
Only the sky turns modern when a jet
veers eastward for Bombay. Below
its powered wings stand sheep and Bedouin.

The sun blinks at me from a donkey's eye
exactly as it blinked eight centuries
ago on tribes of Arabs armed to purge
the last crusader from Jerusalem.
How many bones survive? How many skulls
did Timurlane leave stacked in pyramids

where Bedouin fork wheat against the wind
and watch it fall. I squint for evidence.
The deadness of the sea near Jericho
unscrolls no secrets, and the sand endures
for wind alone to sift and re-arrange
and blow the smell of Briton, Frenchman, Turk

and Mongol to the sun. The time is what
it was when Sarah laughed the angel
back to God. The shepherds wait for Christ. The tribes
of Canaan graze their camels near the road
I conquer like a new crusader armed
with film and cigarettes. Nursed on the blood

of Europe's cross and Europe's rack, I search
for what was here before the world moved west.
A donkey blinks. Bedouin cane their sheep.
A child cries until his mother plumps

her breast against him, thumbs the nipple firm
and plugs the blind mouth mute as history.

Splitting

Unchanged, my whiskersnow of salt
   and pepper in the sink, the shaver
   shearing my chill cheek warm,
   a palmweight of buzzering.
                           With half
   my face to do, a higher power
   sizzles my razor mute.
                        Only
   my passport knows me now.
My mirror shows me half-American,
   half-Adam . . .
                        Beyond my balcony
   all Zurich rises to a signature
   of skyline.
                  Half here, half home,
   half shaven, half asleep, I could be
   watching Cairo, Istanbul, Madrid,
   Beirut.
               A pigeon waves goodbye
   with both its wings and swerves
   for France.
                   My western stare
   outflies it to the Spanish coast,
   the sea and, all at once,
   the States, the States!
                              What is it
   to be gone but never gone?
What leaves me more American
   in Zurich than in Pennsylvania?
For answers I might interview
   those voyagers who've docked with God
   or be myself in different
   hemispheres at once.

                    The Tartars
understood.
                    Away from home,
they kept their jackboots double-soled
with China's soil—so, no matter
where they walked, they walked on China.

Anticipating Yesterday, Remembering Tomorrow

A white stern-wheeler slides
　　downriver for Ohio.
　　　　　　　　　　Its paddles
　　plow the river rough until
　　they seem to falter and reverse.
I've seen the same illusion
　　in the backward-spinning tires
　　of a car accelerating forward,
　　props revolving clockwise
　　counterclockwise, trains departing
　　from a town departing from a train
　　departing.
　　　　　　　To break the spell,
　　I focus on the stern-wheel's hub
　　and slide into a memory of Paris . . .
At Notre Dame a life
　　I seemed to know preceded me.
On Montparnasse I told myself
　　I must have come that way
　　before I came that way.
No matter where I walked,
　　I kept retreating into what
　　came next.
　　　　　　　Even the Seine
　　deceived me with its waves blown
　　west, its current coasting east . . .
The wheel I watch keeps wheeling
　　me behind, ahead, around.
I clutch my lashes to the wind
　　and wait.
　　　　　　　When I release,
　　I know a place I've never seen.

I see a time I've known
   forever.
        Is it tomorrow, yesterday,
  today?
      I drink a breath.
I breathe my life away.

The First and Only Sailing

Your shores diminish.
                    You learn
    the doom of sailors drifting
    south on ice islands.
What echoes shall you code
    to float the sea?
                    When Manolete
    got it from Islero in Linares,
    he rose again as four
    stone matadors in Córdoba.
Likewise Philippe-Auguste,
    who paid his bodyguards with whores
    to keep them loyal.
                    This side
    of memory, you fight the killing
    tides to death for etchings
    on a rock, for life.
                    As for
    the Happy Isles?
                    Let dreamers
    dock there.
                    Believe in such,
    and you'll believe that Essex,
    More, and Mary of Scotland
    kidded the chopper on their climb
    to God.
                    Settle for the whirlpool
    and the cliff.
                    Mermaidens, naked
    at the nipples and below, still
    mate with sailors in their sleep.
And who escapes from sleep?
Waken, and you wage one ship

against the aces of the sea.
Weaken, and the bait of Faust's bad
  wager waits you.
                    Worsen,
and the winds of old indulgence
overtake you.
                    You face them
as you'd face, years afterward,
a girl you kissed and fondled
in a park but never married.
Becalmed, you make your peace
  with dreams.
                    Expect nothing,
and anything seems everything.
Expect everything, and anything
  seems nothing.
                    To live
you leave your yesterselves
to drown without a funeral.
You chart a trek where no
  one's sailed before.
                    You rig.
You anchor up.
                    You sail.

Don Juan's Dream of Near and Far Misses

Your wenching done, you dreamed
  alive your score of paramours:
  she with the whore's lips, she
  from the shore, she with the tanned
  hips, she with real panthers
  staring from her eyes, she
  of the whips and mirrors . . .
                  All
  these you numbered to your skills
  like scalps or notches on a rifle
  stock or stenciled emblems
  of the sun across a fuselage.
Was every girl herself
  or who you dreamed she was?
In Montreal she whispered no,
  no, no, no, no.
             In Alexandria
  she plucked her eyebrows in the nude.
In Rome she never gave
  her name.
           Each time you found
  and took her, she became herself
  anew in someone else.
              Was she
  Yvonne, who never kissed by day,
  or Evelyn, who tangoed you to death?
And what of the twins from Spain?
You offered Ava Eva's ring
  engraved with Eva's name
  on Ava's anniversary.
             When trouble
  doubled, you resolved to choose
  the mate who'd save you from yourself.

Docile you would have her, schooled
  in deference, religious to a point
  but not averse to dalliance.
She of the king's inheritance?
Already spoken for.
                  She
  without attachments?
                     Dying
  in Lugano.
              She who had called
  you casual?
               Your letter came back
  burned . . .
             At last the Home for Old
  Lotharios admitted you.
                  Nuns
  assisted you with slippers, pills
  and liniments.
             You saw fresh
  universes in their faces, not two
  the same but all beyond you.
By night you learned again
  that loins were loins.
                Blinder
  than revenge, they made their own
  decisions.
           You showered in ice water,
  practiced Zen, saltpetered
  all your meals.
           Hair-shirted
  in your cell, you vowed before
  the god of all lost loves
  that you would never take
  that road again, that you
  would take that road never

again, that you would take never
that road again.
Halfway down
the road, you kept repeating that.

Waiting for Zero

Confirming that the avant-garde
   can't wait for history, gray Hemingway
   reached Paris seven days before
   the Liberation.
                    With Nazis near
   the Place Vendome, he freed
   his moveable feast and waited
   for the troops . . .
                  Like Hemingway you wait
   for snow before a January second
   masquerading as the first of May.
The maple buds almost believe it.
Stallion dung around a pear tree
   thaws into its pasture smell
   again.
              Even a buried crocus
   lets its periscope break ground.
So far, no snow.
             Whether
   it will come or go is in
   the winds of Canada.
                But you . . .
You act as if it's here.
               Your blood's
   already down to three below.
Your shoulders chill and heighten
   in the winds to come.
              Remembering
   your future as a fact, you turtle up
   like any seed beneath the snow
   or like a snoozing black bear
   in the hills and wait for Easter,
   wait for history . . .

But just suppose
the wait's too long and troublesome.
Or else suppose that Easter's
not enough—or not at all.
Which brings you back to Hemingway
in Idaho in 1961.
His feast
no longer moveable, his hunter's
eyes too sick to see, his future
certain to grow worse, he faced
the choice of waiting for the end
or not.
At last he thought
ahead of how it felt to be
the first to Paris.
Then,
he held the muzzle cold
between his eyes and shot.

A City Made Sacred Because
Your Son's Grandfather Died in It

Your father in a wheelchair slouches
    steeply to his stroked-out side.
Your son wheels for the final
    time his final grandfather.
And you, who've walked this street
    so many times you know
    the slope and crack of every
    sidewalk square, just walk
    behind.
                You ask your son
    (or is it just your son?)
    to slow things down.
Your father flicks his good
    right hand to say he can't
    accept but won't deny what's
    happened, that not accepting
    what is unacceptable is all
    life meant or means to him.
You want to hold his other
    hand and squeeze it back
    to life until the doctors
    and their facts relent.
                    The doctors
    and their facts go on.
                    So do
    the unaffected riders in the numbered
    buses.
            So does the whole
    city that becomes no more
    than just a place to live
    and die in now.

The more you walk,
the less you know the street
you knew.
The less you know,
the more the curbs become
opposing shores.
The street
is suddenly the river no man
steps in twice or finally outswims.
Midway between your father
and your son, you feel yourself
drawn in and on and under.

The Bearing

Heavy from her steady bellying,
   the mare comes due.
                    No memory
   of ten Kentuckies or the horse farms
   east of Buffalo prepares you
   for the silk of that first fur.
You've seen the Easter foals stilting
   in toy gallops by their almost
   inattentive mothers.
                    You've known
   from watching what the breeding
   of Arabia will hone from all
   that spindliness: in weeks the fetlocks
   shapelier; in months the girth below
   the withers sinewed like a harp;
   in years the stance and prancing
   that will stop a crowd.
But now the colt's nose nudging
   for horsemilk nullifies a dream
   to come of stallions.
                    Now
   it is enough to know that something
   can arrive so perfectly and stand
   upright among so many fallen
   miracles and, standing, fill
   the suddenly all-sacred barn
   with trumpets and a memory of kings.

Only the New Branches Bloom

Denying what it means to doubt,
   this year's forsythias unfold
   and flood the air with yellow
   answers.
           They say it's time
I opened up, time I learned
French, time I liked less
and loved more, time
I listened to the sun, time
I made time.
           Why not?
Can days of making sense
   of days that make no sense
   make sense?
           If nothing's sure
but nothing's sure, then reading
Montesquieu must wait.
Preparing for my enemies must
   wait.
         And gravity the hurrier
must wait because forsythias
are happening.
          They make me
turn my back on forts,
insurance policies, inoculations,
wire barbed or braided,
bodyguards and all the folderol
of fear.
         They say that this
year's blossoms will outlive

the lasting death of Mars.
There are no flowers on the stars.

For Grace (7/19/78)

The Toys

Wing to wing, they bake
  in weather that can sizzle bacon
  on their stars.
              Fighters, bombers,
trainers—Arizona stores them all
  unrusting in a prophecy of yesterday.
West by half the Pacific, the holy
  salvage of another *Arizona*
  consecrates Pearl Harbor like a church.
If wreckages were pages, nothing
  could book them.
              Cain's garbage
mines the Baltic, fouls
  forty years of bracken near
  Cassino, spoils Guam's lagoon.
What were these havocs to their crews
  but new toys for an old game?
As facts left over from a fact,
  they speak for history ahead
  of all that history remembers
  to predict about the tactics of our kind.
Cain's rock and rocket
  leave us nothing new to find.
In North America the oldest skull's
  a woman's, brained from behind.

The Next Time You Were There

After Paris, every city's just
   another town.
                Elephants could roam
the Metro, Marly's horses
could invade the Tuileries, wishbone
arches on the Seine could shatter
under traffic, and Parisians could
refuse to estivate in August . . .
Appearing every day in Paris
   would be Haussmann's Paris still.
Abroad, you'd like to die the way
   you live in Paris—telescoping four
days into three, believing that your best
is just ahead, protesting
that you need more time, more time,
protesting to the end.
                And past
   the end . . .
             But you exaggerate.
This capital you share with France
   is just another web—somewhere
to breathe and board and be.
You bring there what you are,
   and what you are is nowhere
any different.
            This makes
the Trocadero just a penny's patch
of grass, the Place de la Concorde
a wide and spindled planisphere,
and St. Germaine-des-Pres another
church.
            Weathering your dreams,
bronze Paris of the doorknobs

turns into the turning stage
called *here* that stays the same
as everywhere right now.

On that
quick stage a man keeps happening.
From Paris to Paris to Paris,
the only life he knows
is anywhere and always coming
true. . . .

His name is *you*.

The Silence at the Bottom of the Well

It's been expecting me so long
   that I feel late.
               Dropped
stones are what it's thirsty for,
and I've come armed . . .
                     I hear
the ghosts of splashes plummet
upward like the tired swallows
of a heart near death.
               If I
could dunk and hoist a bucket,
I would taste what mountain
brooks remember of the snow.
Instead, I whisper down
   my name, my name, my name
   and listen as it yoyos
   in a rounding echo back,
   back, back . . .
              Below the parapet
the swirling walls dive
farther down than I can dream.
Deeper, where night and water
   meet, the moon of the assassins
   waits for yesterday and never sleeps.

PART TWO
Silence Spoken Here

Maps for a Son Are Drawn as You Go

I say what Lindbergh's father
   said to Lindbergh: "One boy's
   a boy; two boys are half
   a boy; three boys are no
   boy at all."
                    Which helps explain
why Lindbergh kept his boyishness
for life, which meant he stayed
himself, which means a lot.
What else is destiny?
                   After
   you learn that governments lie
   and happiness is undefinable
   and death has no patience,
   you'll understand me.
                  Meanwhile
   the ignorant but well informed
   will try to keep you mute
   as a shut book.
              Forecasters of the best
   and worst will hurry to retreat
   infallibly into the future.
                 Ministers
   who talk on cue with God
   will weigh you down like serious
   furniture.
             Assume that what
   you lose to such distractions
   you will gain in strength.
By then you'll learn that all
   you know will help you less
   than how you think.

                    The rest
is memory, and memory's the graveyard
of the mind as surely as tomorrow
is its myth.
                    Nowhere but the time
at hand is when you'll see
that God's geometry is feast
enough.
                    Within the world's
closed circles, everything's
the sum of halves that rhyme.
From coconuts to butterflies
  to lovers knotted on the soft
  battlefield of any bed, the halves
  add up to one, and every
  one remembers where it came
  from as a trumpet note
  recalls the song it was a part of
  and the listeners who heard it
  and were changed.
                    What Lindbergh's
father meant and what I mean
are two roads to the same
country.
          Knowing how long
it takes us to be young, he left
his son some clues to get
his bearings by.
                    And so do I.

Silence Spoken Here

What absence only can create
  needs absence to create it.
Split by deaths or distances,
  we all survive like exiles
  from the time at hand, living
  where love leads us for love's
reasons.
          We tell ourselves
  that life, if anywhere, is there.
Why isn't it?
          What keeps us
  hostages to elsewhere?
             The dead
  possess us when they choose.
The far stay nearer than we know
  they are.
          We taste the way
  they talk, remember everything
  they've yet to tell us, dream
  them home and young again
  from countries they will never leave.
With friends it's worse and better.
Together, we regret the times
  we were apart.
          Apart, we're
  more together than we are
  together.
          We say that losing
  those we love to living
  is the price of loving.
          We say
  such honest lies because
  we must—because we have

no choices.
                    Face to face
we say them, but our eyes
have different voices.

No Is the Father of Yes

I'm tired of living for tomorrow's
    headlines, tired of explanations,
    tired of letters that begin "Dear
    patriot . . ." or else "You may
    already be the winner of . . ."
I'm near the point where nothing's
    worth the time.
                            The causes
    I believe in rarely win.
The men and women I admire
    most are quietly ignored.
What's called "the infinite
    progression of the negative" assumes
    if I can count to minus seven,
    I can count to minus seven
    million, which means the bad
    can certainly get worse, and that
    the worse can certainly, et cetera . . .
Regardless, I believe
    that something in me always was
    and will be what I am.
I make each day my revolution.
Each revolution is a wheel's full
    turn where nothing seems the same
    while everything's no different.
I want to shout in all the dialects
    of silence that the world we dream
    is what the world becomes,
    and what the world's become
    is there for anyone's re-dreaming.
Even the vanishing of facts
    demands a consecration: the uncolor
    of champagne, the way that presidential

signatures remind me of a heartbeat's
dying scrawl across a monitor,
the languages that earlobes speak
when centered by enunciating pearls,
the sculpture of a limply belted
dress, the instant of bite
when grapes taste grape.
                              The range
of plus is no less infinite
than minus . . .
                    I learn that going
on means coming back
and looking hard at just one thing.
That rosebush, for example.
A single rose on that bush.
The whiteness of that rose.
                              A petal
of that whiteness.
                    The tip
of that petal.
                    The curl of that tip.
And just like that the rose
in all its whiteness blooms
within me like a dream so true
that I can taste it.
                    And I do.

The Quiet Proofs of Love

When your son has grown up, treat him like your brother.
—Arab proverb

Don't wait for definitions.
                    I've had
  my fill of aftertalk
  and overtalk, of meanings that don't
  mean, of words not true
  enough to be invisible, of all
  those Januaries of the mind when
  everything that happens happens
  from the eyebrows up.
                    If truth
  is in the taste and not
  the telling, give me whatever
  is and cannot be again—
  like sherbet on the tongue, like love. . . .
Paris defined is Paris
  lost, but Paris loved
  is always Orly in the rain,
  broiled pork and chestnuts
  near the Rue de Seine,
  the motorcade that sped de Gaulle
  himself through Montparnasse.
                 Long live
  the fool who said, "Show me
  a man who thinks, I'll show
  you a man who frowns."
                Which
  reminds me of Andrew learning
  to count by twos and asking,
  "Where is the end of counting?"

Let's settle for the salt and pepper
    of the facts.
                Oranges don't parse,
and no philosopher can translate
shoulders in defeat or how
it feels when luck's slim arrow
stops at you or why lovemaking's
not itself until it's made.
Let's breathe like fishermen who sit
    alone together on a dock
    and let the wind do all
    the talking.
                That way we'll see
that who we are is what
we'll be hereafter.
                We'll learn
the bravery of trees that cannot
know "the dice of God
are always loaded."
                We'll think
of life as one long kiss
since talk and kisses never mix.
We'll watch the architecture
    of the clouds create themselves
    like flames and disappear like laughter.

The First Sam Hazo at the Last

A minor brush with medicine
  in eighty years was all
  he'd known.
                   But this was different.
His right arm limp and slung,
  his right leg dead to feeling
  and response, he let me spoon him
  chicken-broth.
                Later he said
without self-pity that he'd like
to die.
          I bluffed, "The doctors
think that therapy might help you
walk again."
             "They're liars,
all of them," he muttered.
                   Bedfast
was never how he hoped to go.
"In bed you think of everything,"
  he whispered with a shrug, "you think
  of all of your life."
              I knew
he meant my mother.
                Without her
he was never what he might have been,
  and everyone who loved him knew it.
Nothing could take her place—
  not the cars he loved to drive,
  not the money he could earn at will,
  not the roads he knew by heart
  from Florida to Saranac, not the two
  replacement wives who never
  measured up.

            Fed now by family
    or strangers, carried to the john,
    shaved and changed by hired help,
    this independent man turned silent
    at the end.
            Only my wife
    could reach him for his private needs.
What no one else could do
    for him, he let her do.
She talked to him and held
    his hand, the left.
                    She helped him
    bless himself and prayed beside him
    as my mother might have done.
"Darling" was his final word
    for her.
            Softly, in Arabic.

Song for the Flies of Fire

The fifty-year-old girl of twenty
   said, "In love it's best
   to be cynical."
                  She'd modeled, acted
in French commercials, and sung
   rock with a group called
   "Soviet Sex."
                  Her eyes were cat's
eyes but without the mystery.
Her smile faded like tired foam
   or like a memory of Berryman,
   who, when all he spoke and wrote
   was poetry, decided he was through.
That's how it ends with some.
Burn fast, burn out . . .
                  Even
   the repenters live clichés
   that guarantee oblivion.
                Grundy,
   who put himself through college
   selling marijuana, prosecutes
   for Justice now in Washington.
Eldridge Cleaver shouts
   like Billy Sunday.
                Nixon's
   cronies milk the lecture
   circuit, publish fiction
   and believe with all their re-born
   might in President Jesus . . .
I think like this while watching
   lightning bugs play midnight
   tag around my house.

Ignite
and pause.
            Ignite and pause—
each one its own Prometheus,
a sun in flight, a type
of Edison.
            They burn like signals
hyphenated by the breath of night.
Each time I think they're burning out
    instead of on, they burn again
    like pulses that will just not die.
Their brightness lightens me.
It's no small thing to bear
    a dawn within you.
                    It's
even more at midnight to create
with nothing but your being
plus a light that tunes the darkness
something like the music of the sky.

Florence by Proxy

October's ochre changes
    everything to Italy.
                    Sunpainted
    walls remember villas
    from Fiesole.
                    I've never seen
    Fiesole.
                Some day I will,
    and it will seem a memory
    of noon in the United States
    when I became a Florentine
    because the sun bewildered me.
Who among the Florentines
    is listening?
                    Who else but me
    who sees in the Italians
    "the human race" that Goethe
    saw . . .
                Today their cops
    are commodores; their Fiats,
    weapons in their whizzing duels
    on the road; their shoes and gloves,
    the very renaissance of calf.
Tribal to the death, they swear
    by their mothers, breastfeed
    their sons wherever, prefer
    their pasta three-fourths cooked,
    and sing whatever whenever . . .
Mistaken for Italian half
    my life, I'm of the tribe.
If it's Italian to speak
    in tears before goodbyes,
    I qualify.

                    If it's Italian
        to choose tomatoes one
        by one, I qualify.
                              If it's
        Italian to laugh when no one
        else is laughing or to whistle
        at the wheel, I qualify.
                              One
        murmur in Italian soothes
        the Florentine in me that French
        confuses, German contradicts,
        and Spanish misses by a hair.
    One murmur, and I feel
        what Goethe felt when Florence
        wounded him with Italy
        for life though Goethe spent
        not quite three hours there.

Kak

Her heroines were Pola Negri,
 Gloria Swanson, and Mae West—
 one for glamour, one for style,
 one for nerve.
                    First on her scale
 of praise came courage of the heart,
 then brains, then something called
 in Arabic "lightbloodedness."
                              All
 birds but owls she loved, all
 that was green and growable,
 including weeds, all operas
 in Italian, the schmaltzier the better. . . .
Lightning she feared, then age
 since people thought the old
 "unnecessary," then living on
 without us, then absolutely nothing.
Each time I'd say some girl
 had perfect legs, she'd tell me
 with a smile, "Marry her legs."
Of if I'd find a project
 difficult, she'd say, "Your mother,
 Lottie, mastered Greek
 in seven months."
                    Or once
 when Maris bested Ruth's
 home runs by one, she said,
 "Compared to Ruth, who's Harris?"
Crying while she stitched my shirt,
 she said, "You don't know
 what to suffer is until
 someone you love is suffering
 to death, and what can you do?"

On principle she told one bishop
    what she thought of him.
On personality she called one
    global thinker temporarily
    insane.
                She dealt a serious
hand of poker, voted
her last vote for Kennedy,
and wished us a son two years
before he came.
                She hoped
that she would never die
in bed.
                And never she did.
"When you and your brother were young,"
    she said, "and I was working,
    then was I happy."
                    And she was.
The folderol of funerals disgusted
    her enough to say, "I'm
    telling no one when
    I die."
                And she didn't.
One night she jotted down
    in longhand on a filing card,
    "I pray to God that I'll be
    with you always."
                And she is.

Another Word for Time

We speak as people in motion
   speak, more sure of what's
   behind us than ahead,
   but going anyway.
                Trying to see
beyond the world we see,
we see that seeing's dangerous.
Our props collapse.
             Religion,
custom, law, the dream
called government . . .
             Nothing
sustains us but our eyes and what
our eyes, by saying nothing,
say.
      No wonder Timmerman
could claim for all of us,
"I'm more at home in subjects
now, not countries."
            Before
the real frontiers, our passports
are invalid.
       They tell us
how we're called but never
who we are, and who we are's
the mystery.
         The pilgrim in us
has no fixed address.
             He roams.
He takes us with him when
   he goes.
         Encowled within
a fuselage, we speed toward

a short tomorrow in another
world.
          We land, speak languages
we almost understand, and trust
in strangers as the best of friends,
and for a time they are.
                    Years
afterward we feel a bond
with them so indestructible
that we're amazed.
              If they
should die, we'd grieve for them
like those old Cuban fishermen
who grieved for Hemingway because
he fished the gulf they fished
and called them friends.
               With nothing
else to offer him, they gave
the bronze propellers of their
very boats for melting to create
his statue in the plaza of Cojimar . . .
For us the best memorials
are what we heard or read
en route.
          "He'd old, but still
in life."
          "Nothing but heart
attack kill Christophine, but why
in that box she so swell up?"
"Cruelty's a mystery and a waste
of pain."
          "I like a dog
that makes you think when you
look at him."

"El Cordobés es
un hombre muy valiente."
                    Each word's
a time.
            Each time's a place.
Each place is where a time
    repeats itself because a word
    returns us there.
                    Crisscrossing
through the universe the way
that lightning diagrams the sky,
we're all companions of the road
at different altitudes.
                    Here
in my speeding house below
the speeding stars, I'm turning
into language from a pen while you're
confiding in some traveler you'll
never see again.
                    The quiet
bronze of words remembers us.
                            It says
we were, we are, we will be.

No Fanfares, No Handshakes, No Salutes

If "life's a dream with doubts
    about itself," the dreaming
    never stops.
                    Regretting
what you did or did not do
or always wished to do adds up
to who you are . . .
                    Piaf pretended
she regretted nothing.
                    One
genius in his epitaph regretted
only he was not "the man
in whose embrace Mathilde Urbach
swooned."
                    One emperor with no
regrets in middle age
regretted having no regrets.
Translated, these examples say
    no life is long enough
    nor cosmopolitan enough nor anything
    enough.
                    If you desire to see
your son's daughter's son's
daughter, you want no less
than anybody wants.
                        Or if you thirst
to visit everywhere in every
hemisphere, you mimic old Batuta's
passion for the next horizon.
Or if you hunger for the maximum,
    you're Faust with all of Faust's
    excesses to remember . . .

                         So much
for dreams.
                    If you want something
to regret, why not regret you never
once opposed some fluent undermen
we manage to elect—the ideology
or sociology or therapy that people
eat as poetry—the arguments
about theology whose final argument
is *who's the boss*—the righteous
tribes for whom the Renaissance might
just as well have never happened?
Why did you never say that one
good student's worth a thousand
senators?
                    Or that one carpenter
outskills the slitherings of advertisers,
diplomats, and other oilers of the word?
Between what you remember
or presume, you're in translation
by whatever keeps translating April
into May, decisions into consequences,
fathers into sons, and you
into whatever.
                    I know
the circumstance.
                    I'm *you,*
and both of us keep planning
for tomorrow while we're turning
into yesterday.
                    What else
can we conclude except we live
and die in place despite
our dreams?

What is our bounty
but the permanent impermanence
of breath, a shared invisibility,
a gift?
            What is our peace
but stopping as we go and talking
for a while of that, just
that, translation to translation?

Who Promised You Tomorrow?

It's time you paganized yourself
  and left all sublimations
  to the dry of soul.
               It's time
  you learned that ears can taste,
  and eyes remember, and the tongue
  and nostrils see like fingertips
  in any dark.
           Think back
  or look around, and all you know
  is what your body taught you:
  lake smoke in the Adirondacks,
  the razor's flame across
  your lathered cheek, language
  that changed to silence or to tears
  when there was nothing more
  to say . . .
          Right here in Cannes
  on the Fourth of July, you watch
  a cornucopia a-swelter in the sun.
A Saudi wife, enrobed
  and cowled like a nun, passes
  a Cannaise in her isosceles
  and thong.
          They stand there
  like opposed philosophies of women,
  history, desire, God,
  and everything you think about
  too much . . .
          The stationed candles
  on the altar of Notre Dame
  de Bon Voyage diminish
  like your future.

                    Anchored
        in the bay, the S. S. *Ticonderoga*
        claims the future's now.
Housing a zillion dollars'
        worth of hardware in her hull,
        she's programmed for the war
        that no one wants.
                    She bristles
        like a ploughshare honed into a sword—
        the ultra-weapon from the ultra-tool.
Basking in the hull of your skin
        that shields the software of yourself
        against the worst, you contemplate
        the carefully united states
        you call your body.
                    Concealed
        or bared, it houses who you are,
        and who you are is why you live,
        and why you live is worth
        the life it takes to wonder how.
Your body's not concerned.
                        It answers
        what it needs with breath, sleep,
        love, sweat, roses,
        children, and a minimum of thought.
It says all wars are waged
        by puritans, and that the war
        nobody wants is history's excuse
        for every war that ever happened. . . .
The gray *Ticonderoga* fires
        a salute of twenty guns
        plus one for independence
        and the men who died to earn it.
Each shot reminds you of the killed
        Americans still left in France.

Before they left their bodies,
   did they think of war or what
   their bodies loved and missed
   the most: a swim at noon,
   the night they kissed a woman
   on her mouth, the times they waited
   for the wind to rise like music,
   or the simple freedom of a walk,
   a waltz, a trip?
                    Under
the sun of Cannes, you hum
your mind to sleep.
                    You tell
yourself that time is one
day long or one long day
with pauses for the moon and stars,
and that tomorrow's sun is yesterday's
today.
          Your body answers
that it knows, it's known
for years, it's always known.

Unto the Islands

Each dawn I slew the sand
   behind Grand Case toward
   the cape where Jackie O
   is building her alternative.
                              Upbeach,
   two naked mermaids snorkel
   through the surf, their backs
   awash with ocean suds, their gleaming
   bottoms, like O'Murphy's, dolphining
   in tandem as their finned feet
   churn.
              A poem I've been planning
   pulls apart.
              The more I mine
   for nouns and fish for verbs
   the more it pulls apart.
                              By noon
   the almost breathing sea assumes
   the fully female languor
   of a woman sleeping naked
   on the beach—her breasts adjusting
   as she turns, her thighs dividing
   like abandonment itself, her mating
   slot so free of shame it shows
   its secret to the sun.
                              I tell
   myself I'm here like Jackie O,
   and for a week it's true.
                              The time
   is always sun o'clock, and every
   day is Sunday.
              The nights
   are stars and coffee and a netted

bed.
        But all around me live
black men with Dutch and French
and Spanish names and blood
so mixed that all the scars
of slavery bleed through.
                    Daily
they show me history in sepia.
That history's defunct and all
the slavers sunk, but still
the only church is Catholic Dutch.
The menus mimic Europe,
and a drunk whose middle name
is Van distributes all the Heinekens
in town.
        But who am I
to criticize?
            An ex-colonial myself,
I can't distinguish custom
in my life from conscience, and I
end half-Calvinist half-hedonist
with nothing to confess but
contradiction.
            Island or mainland,
what's the difference?
                    Until
a poem I cannot deny denudes
me into life, I'm just another
pilgrim passing through the obvious.
I need a true alternative
where now is never long
enough to write down what
I know.
        Instead I stay a tan
away from who I was a hemisphere

ago.
      I'm western history
revisited.
        I'm souvenirs and sun
revisited.
        I pay my way and go.

The Real Reason for Going Is Not Just to Get There

Killarney's maps are for the unredeemed.
The hidden land awaits the stumblers
   and the temporarily confused who find
   their destinations as they go.
In Dingle there's a history
   bone-final as the faith
   that founded Gallarus.
                    All
   that remains is what was there
   when Gallarus began: God,
   man, sheep, and stone
   and stone and stone.
               Dingles
   ago the starvers saw their lips
   turn green from chewing grass
   before they famished in their beds.
Their hovels bleach like tombs
   unroofed and riven by the sea.
If only all the stones were beige
   or marble-white . . .
             Their fading
grays seem unforgiving as a fate
   that only wit or tears
   or emigration can defeat.
Sheep graze over graves.
Loud gulls convene on garbage
   dumps.
        In Galway, Cashel
and Tralee, I fish the air
   for what it is that makes
   the Irish Irish.
          Is it Seamus
speaking Sweeney's prayer

in Howth and telling me of Hopkins,
"the convert," buried in Glasnevin?
Is it how it sounds to sing
the music in a name: Skibbereen,
Balbriggan, Kilbeggan, Bunratty,
Listowel, Duncannon, Fermanagh
and Ballyconneely?
                              Is it Joyce's
map of metaphors that makes
all Dublin mythical as Greece?
Is it cairns of uniambic and unrhyming
rocks transformed by hand
into the perfect poem of a wall?
Is it the priest near death
who whispered, "Give my love
to Roscommon, and the horses
of Roscommon?"
                              Is it because
the Irish pray alike for "Pope
John Paul, our bishop Eamon, and
Ned O'Toole, late of Moycullen?"
Inside God's house or out
their sadder smiles say the world,
if given time, will break your heart.
With such a creed they should
believe in nothing but the wisdom
of suspicion.
                      Instead they say,
"Please God," and fare ahead
regardless of the odds to show
that life and God deserve at least
some trust, some fearlessness, some courtesy.

For Anne Mullin Burnham

A Crossing

Boarding this ship of Paul
    the mariner, we bring and find
    our bearings here.
                 West
    of our birth and east of death,
    we sail from southern porches
    to the true north of God. . . .
Though churches built like ships
    or crosses rise no more,
    we still can tell within these
    walls the time of all cathedrals.
Their bells and trumpets summon
    us to be what we can be
    for the believing.
                 Their altars
    prophesy that men who build
    what will outlive them build
    like that first sailor of the Lord
    who christened for the Christ
    he never saw the whole world
    west of Byblos. . . .
                 If where
    we live the best is when
    we love the most, we sail
    like Paul as far as we can love.
That love's the same in Antioch
    or Chartres or in this sheer
    and steepled prayer.
               The compass
    of this cross shall lead us there.

The World That Lightning Makes

Under an upside-down
   and sooty ocean, I steer
   through summer thunder
   and the straight prose of rain.
A dashboard voice from Washington
   talks war in Lebanon . . .
                     Bursting
   like rocketry, a scar of fire
   slashes down the sky.
                 It noons
   the night and shocks me
   to a crawl.
           My car's a shelter
   under siege.
            The mean buttons
   of approaching headlights
   change into the always searching
   always aiming eyes of condors.
The lashing rainfall wails
   in Arabic for this Guernica
   in Beirut . . .
           I think of Lorca
   who believed the lightning-worlds
   of love and poetry could have
   no enemies.
           He never dreamed
   of lightning-chevrons on black
   shirts, lightning-wars
   and lightning-zigzags crayoned
   on a map that sparked a war
   that scarred a generation . . .
               This generation's
   condors thunder on another

Spain.
      The rain's a litany
of Lorcas bulldozed into pits.
The world from Washington is no one's
  and the world's.
          Viva la muerte!

Whatever Happened to Defiance?

People you will never want to know
   are telling you to vote, enlist,
   invest, travel to Acapulco,
   buy now and pay later, smoke,
   stop smoking, curb your dog,
   remember the whale and praise
   the Lord.
               Like windshield wipers
they repeat themselves.
                     Because
they tell but never ask, you learn
to live around them just to live.
You understand why Paul Gauguin
   preferred Tahiti to the bourgeoisie
   of France.
               But then Tahiti's
not the answer anymore,
and frankly never was.
                 This leaves
you weighing Schulberg's waterfront
philosophy: "You do it to him
before he does it to you."
Reactionary, you admit, but nature's
   way, the way of this world
   where he who wins is always
   he who loses least and last. . . .
But if you're bored by triumph
   through attrition, imitate you may
   the strategy of Puck.
                  Listen
carefully to all solicitations, smile
and respond in classical Greek.
It's devious, but then it gives

you time to smell the always
breathing flowers.
                    Or to watch
dissolve into the mystery of coffee
the faceless dice of sugar
cubes.
            Or say just how
remarkable it is that every
evening somewhere in this world
a play of Shakespeare's being staged
with nothing to be won but excellence.

To All My Mariners in One

Forget the many who talk
  much, say little, mean
  less and matter least.
                  Forget
we live in times when broadcasts
of Tchaikovsky's Fifth precede
announcements of the death
of tyrants.
             Forget that life
for governments is priced
war-cheap but kidnap-high.
Our seamanship is not with such.
From port to port we learn
  that "depths last longer
  than heights," that years are
  meant to disappear like wakes,
  that nothing but the sun stands
  still.
       We share the sweeter
alphabets of laughter and the slower
languages of pain.
             Common
as coal, we find in one another's
eyes the quiet diamonds
that are worth the world.
               Drawn
  by the song of our keel, what
  are we but horizons coming true?
Let others wear their memories
  like jewelry.
           We're of the few
  who work apart so well
  together when we must.

                    We speak
cathedrals when we speak
and trust no promise but
the pure supremacy of tears.
                    What
more can we expect?
                    The sea's
blue mischief may be waiting
for its time and place, but still
we have the stars to guide us.
We have the wind for company.
We have ourselves.
                    We have
a sailor's faith that says
not even dying can divide us.

Soldiers Despite Ourselves

Downstairs a trumpeter is playing
  Gershwin badly but somehow
  truer that way.
           The squat
chimney of my pipe keeps offering
smoke signals to the moon.
The sea-waves glitter like a zillion
  nickels . . .
         Two wars ago
the battle of the Riviera happened
here.
        Two wars ago
the author of *The Little Prince*
flew southward from this coast
and crashed at sea without a trace.
That's how I tell the time
  these days—by wars, the madness
  of wars.
        I think of Mussolini,
who believed each generation
needed war to purify its blood.
He leaned on history to show
  that life's unlivable except
  through death.
         I palm the ashes
from my pipe.
       To hell
with Mussolini.
       I'll take
bad Gershwin to a bullet
any time.
      To hell with history.
The moon's manna on the sea

outshines the glory that was Greece.
To hell with those who say
   the earth's a battleground we're doomed
   to govern with a gun.
                          Because
of them we have to fight to live.
But win or lose, they've won
   since fighting proves they're right.
Why ask if they outnumber us
   or not?
            It just takes one.

Matador

He killed dying, and he died killing.
—Translation of the headline announcing
the death of Manolete, August 28, 1948

Are my eyes open, Doctor? I can't see.
—Last words of Manolete

The photographs survive.
                        He stands
at sentinel's attention in his suit
of lights.
            His cape encowls him
like a crimson wing.
                        Kneeling
before the snout or kissing
the horn of a bled and broken
bull he thought undignified.
                        Instead
he faced the black fury
of the beast at full strength,
steering him from miss to miss
until the sacrifice.
                        His art
was not to fight but to conduct
the bull the way a maestro
might conduct an orchestra.
                        With death
as close as God or love,
he worked his cape like a baton
and never moved his feet . . .
He never moved his feet.
No wonder they revere his melancholy
    courage to this very day

in Córdoba, Madrid and Mexico.
And they have reason.
                              Even
the ones who hate the spectacle
revere the man who braved so
much without a backward step.
Forget the fame, the mistress
and the fortune in pesetas.
                         Can these
explain why someone heeds
a calling that allows as many
victories as possible but only
one defeat?
              What each of us
evades until the end, he faced
twelve hundred times alone
by choice.
              Twelve hundred times . . .
His final bull surprised him
even as he stabbed and left him
crumpled, gored and bleeding
on the sand.
                 That memory
is ours to swallow like the bread
of sorrow and the wine of contradiction.
It shows that valor's a delaying
action after all.
                      If done
with grace, we praise the artistry
and skill.
                  If not, we say
the unexpected is the way
that life can always overrule us
in the name of life.

And life
can spare.
And life can kill.

To Stop and Be Stopped in Lourmarin

Monsieur Camus, you gave
  the stone of our absurdity a name.
Daily we roll it to our graves.
There's no reprieve.
            Regardless,
  you believed we'd never come
  alive until we chose to live
  without appeal for living's
  sake alone.
        Such choices
  put self-murder in its place.
Later, you wrote that we are best
  when we rebel—against the casual
  unfairness of the world, against
  acceptance and the cowardice
  it hides, against rebellion
  itself.
      Rebelling with your pen,
  you called the evil of our age
  our willingness to kill within
  the law.
      You cited war
  and punishments called capital.
Today you'd add the legal
  murders of the undesirable,
  the old, the differently religious,
  or the merely different and the not
  yet born.
      But why go on?
You wrote as poets write.
You showed our shame to us
  and stopped us like a stroke.
For you real justice meant

how daringly we face the unavoidable
while struggling for the unattainable.
Because your words defined
   our century the way a hub
   defines a wheel, I've come
   with other pilgrims here to pay
   my last respects.
                     Standing
   beside your name and life-dates
   nicked in rock, I disagree
   with history.
                     Your elegists believed
   your sudden death by accident
   near Villeblevin was premature.
If you could speak, you would
   have said that chance makes
   nothing premature, that lifetimes
   never end the way they should . . .
But what is all this disquisition
   to the life of Lourmarin?
                     The flowers
   of the sun return its Cyclops
   stare the way they always have.
Sweet lavender grows wild
   across your grave.
                     The vineyards
   turn the wind to musk.
                     And all
   the never-to-be-duplicated clouds
   look undisturbed and indestructible.

The Song of the Horse

My father said, "All horses
  when they run are beautiful."
I think of that each time
  I watch Arabians in silhouette,
  the clobbering drays, the jet
  stallions that policemen rein,
  the stilting foals and colts, the sometimes
  bumping always pumping rumps
  of geldings harnessed to a rig.
They prance through war and history:
  "Without a horse the Mongols
  never could have conquered Europe."
And tragedy: "A horse, a horse,
  my kingdom for a horse!"
And sport: "Five minutes
  of hard polo will exhaust
  the strongest horse on earth."
Unsaddled and afoot, how far
  could Cossack, cowboy, Indian,
  and cavalier have gone?
                 What made
so many generals and emperors
  prefer their portraiture on horseback?
What simulacrum but a horse
  succeeded where Achilles failed?
And where did John put hatred,
  famine, pestilence, and war
  but on the backs of horses?
                  And that's
  not all.
      Pegasus still says
to gravity that poetry's none
other than a horse with wings.

It's not a question of intelligence.
Horses, like poetry, are not
    intelligent—just perfect
    in a way that baffles conquest,
    drama, polo, plow,
    and shoe.
            So poem-perfect
    that a single fracture means
    a long, slow dying in the hills
    or, if man's around, the merciful
    aim an inch below the ear.
But when they run, they make
    the charge of any boar at bay,
    the prowl of all the jungle
    cats, the tracking beagle,
    or the antelope in panic seem
    ignoble.
            Just for the sake
    of the running, the running, the running
    they run . . .
            And not another
    animal on two or four
    or forty legs can match
    that quivering of cords beneath
    their pelts, the fury in their manes,
    the hooves that thump like rapid
    mallets on the earth's mute drum,
    the exultation of the canter and the gallop
    and the rollick and frolic and the jump.

Not Even Solomon . . .

Whatever you can buy's not valuable
    enough, regardless of the cost.
What can't be bought's invaluable.
Not just the white freedom
    of a rose, sparrows in their soaring
    circuses, that girl from Amsterdam
    so tanly tall in Montfleury,
    harbors at noon with clouds
    above them pillowing like snow
    and absolutely still.
                        I'm talking
love.
        I'm talking love
and poetry and everything that's true
of each and interchangeably of both.
Randomly free, they leave
    us grateful to no giver
    we can name.
                    They prove what cannot
    last can last forever even
    when we say it's lost . . .
Some losers ache like Aengus
    or like Leila's madman, pining
    for a time so briefly given
    and so quickly gone.
                        Bereft,
    they raise their anguish into songs
    that give a tongue to wounds
    that never heal.
                    In every song
    they imitate those troubadours
    whose poems have outlived
    their lives.

93

Forget how far
they went in school, their ages,
or their kin.
Whatever wanted
to be said and wanted only them
to say it made them what
they are.
It turned them
into words that we can share
like bread and turn into ourselves.
They asked, as I am asking now,
for some less unforgiving way
to say it, and there isn't.
Or if what happened once
might be repeated, and it can't.
Or if another's poets words
would say it better, and they don't.
Of if this cup could pass
and spare them poetry and all
its contradictions, and it won't.

PART THREE
The Most You Least Expect

For Bill

No one but you could write,
    "Our Father Who Art in Heaven
    can lick their Father Who Art
    in Heaven."
                        After we laughed,
    we saw all wars from Troy
    to Vietnam in those two lines.
You had the gift of turning
    smiles into thoughts in such
    a quiet, Quaker way.
                        And yet
    the saying stayed so casual
    and conversational and untranslatably
    Bill Stafford.
                        I still remember
    when we read in Michigan
    together—you from a spiral
    notebook crammed with short
    poems in longhand.
                        Listening,
    I strove to spot where the poems
    stopped, and the prose began.
I never found the seam . . .
When you wrote *Someday, Maybe*
    what was it you were telling us?
If it was loss, that day
    was yesterday.
                        You finished polishing
    a poem that would be your last,
    stood up to help your wife,
    and fell like a soldier.
                        As endings
    go, that seems regrettably

acceptable.
              But why does it
remind me of the silence following
a poem's final line?
I want the poem to go on
    forever, but it doesn't.
                    And it does.

Understory

It's not that sometimes I forget.
I'm told that everybody does.
What troubles me is how
   whatever I've forgotten trebles
   in importance the more I keep
   forgetting it.
              Some word . . .
                         Some place . . .
Today a student from the Class
   of Way Back When
   seemed certain I'd remember him
   by name.
             I tried and tried
   before I had to ask . . .
                   Though students
and ex-students are my life,
I must admit that I remember
most of the best, all
of the worst, many who have left
this world and not that many
of the rest.
              It leaves me wondering . . .
Is memory a beast that sheds
   its baggage as it goes?
Are facts by definition destined
   for oblivion?
             Or is it absolute
that what I can't forget no matter
how I try is all that's worth
remembering?
             I know a mother
of four sons who mixes up
their names.

Ollie is Bennett.
Bennett is Drew.
                Drew
is Christopher.
                Facing one,
she'll travel down the list before
she'll ask, "Tell me your name,
dear boy."
                Outsiders realize
they're all one boy to her,
regardless of their names.
                        She knows
them by their souls.
                        That reassures me.

For JoAnn Bevilacqua-Weiss

Putting Away the Lost Summer

The swing's unslung and winter-waxed,
  the mint leaves waiting to be sieved
  to salt, the hose unscrewed
  and coiled like a rattler in the shed.
As usual the ripening figs
  will blacken at first frost
  exactly as they did last year
  when all the talk was war.
This year the human harvest
  makes the war seem dim:
  one suicide, three deaths, one
  shock, one disappointment, and a swindle.
Each one bequeathed its epitaph:
  "Your letter was a narrow bridge
  to the rest of my life."
                    "He didn't
recognize me, Sam—his own
sister."
          "I'll stay until he's well
or else not here anymore."
Remembering, I see how much
  can never be the way it was,
  despite appearances.
                    Philosophy's
no help.
         Religion's even less.
And poetry does nothing but re-live
  what's lost without redeeming it
  like life's predictable revision
  of itself.
          What's left
but learning to survive with wounds?
Or studying the fate of figs

before the unexpected chill,
not knowing in advance how many
or how few will be destroyed
or toughened when it comes . . .
Playing for time, I occupy
myself with chores and tools,
uncertain if the lot I've chosen
is a gambler's or a coward's or a fool's.

The University of All Smiles

The sleek and Anglo-Saxon Christ
  on all the calendars looks
  vaguely like an ad for beards.
WGOD is loud with Armageddon,
  cattle prices and the songs
  of Brother Benjamin.
                    Splayed
on my guestroom desk, a Bible,
  bound in lavender leather,
  crinkles with onionskin psalms.
In the face of so much virtue,
  what can I do but watch
  my step?
              Everyone says
hello, even the joggers.
Everyone smiles, even
  the frowners.
                Everyone shows
what it's like to be saved, even
the jokers . . .
              Gardens without
a snake bring out the Holmes
in me.
          I sniff for a little
conspicuous vice, but here
it's hidden like pornography in Mecca.
Call me obtuse, but I'm on guard
  when good and bad don't co-exist
  as I distrust elections where
  there's no dissent.
              I'm more
at peace with Dante's sinner-saints
than all the kindergartens of Angelico.

So, Brother Benjamin, sing on.
The world may end at three
   o'clock tomorrow afternoon,
   and all who smoke cigars
   may be the devil's spawn.
My world begins and ends
   each time I breathe.

                           I smoke
cigars.
          I sing a different song.

The Most You Least Expect

You think of photographic paper
  drowning in developer.
                    Slowly
  the whiteness darkens into forms.
Shadows become a face;
  the face, a memory; the memory,
  a name.
          The final clarity
  evolves without a rush
  until it's there.
            It's like
  your struggle to remember
  what you know you know
  but just can't quite recall.
No matter how you frown,
  the secret stays beyond you.
You reach.
        It moves.
              You reach
  again.
        Again it moves.
It's disobedience itself, but still
  it wants so much to be regained
  by you, only by you.
             Later,
  when it lets itself be known,
  you wonder how you ever could
  have lost so obvious a thing.
And yet you take no credit
  for retrieving it.
            It came to you
  on its own terms, at its
  own time.

You woke, and it
was there like love or luck
or life itself and asked
no more of you than knowing
it by name.
            The name is yours
to keep.
            You burn to share
this sudden and surprising gold
with everyone.
                    You feel the glee
of being unexpectedly complete
and sure and satisfied and chosen.

When Nothing's Happening, Everything's Happening

There's something "old school"
  about you, Charles, and that's
  what I admire most.
                  You still
  believe in friendship, manners,
  duty, generosity and Launceston.
I've never been to Launceston.
Your postcards proffer me a proper
  Norman town in Cornwall
  topped by a castle.
               I'm told
  that all your townsmen know
  who Mr. Causley is, and why not?
You schooled three generations there
  for half a century.
             That keeps
  you dearer to your kin than all
  your books.
           But it was books
  that paired us for a shared recital
  under Shakespeare's shadow.
                After
Stratford, it was letters, phone
  calls, meeting once in Washington
  and once in Pittsburgh.
              Now
  it's messages through mutual friends.
Or poetry—especially your dream
  about your parents on a picnic.
Dead for decades, they're sharing tea
  and stoppering a milk jug
  with a "screw of paper."

They wave
for you to join them in a feast
that's a reprise of Eden.
They're young
and happy and in love, and the Cornish
sky shines brighter than the borealis
through your last (and lasting) words. . . .
Your letters last as well, and that
includes the jotted postscripts
on the outside flaps.
It's so damn
good to read what keeps alive
what's dearest to a man.
It shows
we're not enslaved to memory
or mere presumption—born liars
both.
It says the present perfect
is the only tense in any tongue,
which means the past is now
whenever poets breathe it
into life again.
So here's
to the poet from Launceston.
And here's
to your paper and ink.
And here's
to the poems borne of your pen
that help us to feel what we think.
Long live the books that you've written,
and long live the books that you'll write
like bread for the dead in the morning
and eyes for the blind at night.

For Charles Causley

Scientia Non Est Virtus

> *The good that I would I do not;*
> *the evil that I would not, that I do.*
> —St. Paul

After a week in Paris you saw
  in a sign a word you'd never
  learned.
            Stopping a passerby,
you asked in French if he
  were French.
              The response in French
could best be rendered as "perhaps. . . ."
A month would pass before
  a laundress asked if many
  in America wrote poetry.
You told her there were thousands.
"But," she insisted, "do you have
  one Baudelaire?"
              Such anecdotes
not only give new meaning
  to nuance but demonstrate
  how ignorance differs from knowledge,
  and knowledge from holy wisdom.
Though ignorance at best means nothing,
  knowledge may stay the fool of villainy,
  while villainy plays weevil to the will.
And what's the will except a wayward
  stallion ridden by our dreams
  to glory or perdition?
              For every
Shakespeare, Lincoln, or Saint Matthew
there's a murderer, liar, reprobate
or whore who mastered the Britannica

but stayed the same.
                         Old or young,
we learn too late that being
good is more than strict adherence
to commandments, laws, or codes,
much more than being well
informed, and light-years more
than all the learning in the world.
What is morality but shunning
    deeds we just can't do even
    when the opportunities present
    themselves?
                         It's reflex
more than choice or reasoning . . .
If that sounds like a substitute
    for ignorance, then ignorance it is.
If it seems paradoxical
    but vaguely possible, it's knowledge.
If it makes sense, it's wisdom.

While Walking on France

Call it the time of bread
   in Cannes: baguettes in stacks
   like ammunition, jumbled croissants,
   and bins of buns and rolls.
At the hotel desk, Sonya
   and Nadeige sing the French
   they speak.
               Madame Antoine,
   whose son Deleuse, Cannonier
   1st Class, died at twenty
   in Algeria, carefully counts coins.
Postcards on the Rue d'Antibes
   remember Gary Cooper, Grace Kelly,
   Bardot, Gabin and Robert Mitchum.
At the Moulin de Mougins a festival
   ago, Sharon Stone bankrolled
   a banquet for AIDS.
               Villas
   in "high" Cannes nestle (yes,
   like nests) in grottoes guarded
   by monitors and bougainvillea.
                   Bentleys,
   Daimlers and Porsches cruise
   the Autoroute as privately
   as hearses for the totally enclosed.
Sepulchrally asprawl on beaches
   loll the supine and the prone,
   their tans proceeding by degrees.
Beside a hotel pool a girl
   strips to one triangular swatch
   to model swimsuits for the trade.
This land where taste is king
   and genuine panache is queen

attracts and puzzles me.
Does French reluctance spring
   from stubbornness or thought?
What prompts French chocolatiers to make
   the package more seductive than the purchase?
Who but these slim-skulled brothers
   of Rimbaud accord great chefs
   a reverence reserved for kings
   or popes?
                Each time that France
   is underfoot I memorize
   but never judge why pigeons
   chortle the only song
   they know, how palms upsurge
   into a fountainhead of leaves,
   or why the twin born last
   in France is legally the elder . . .
As men essentialize and women
   existentialize, I focus on ideas
   and ignore the facts.
                The facts,
I come to see, are France.
                  They state
their own philosophy.
                The more
I know of it, the less
I understand.
            The less I understand,
the more I know that some
confusions never yield to reason.

Cezanne's Atelier near Aix

It's as he left it, or as it
   left him after he painted it.
A sprawl of dappled quince,
   three pipes, and two pairs
   of spectacles command a tabletop.
A crumpled tam relaxes
   at the opposite end.
               I think
a lamp centers the two,
but I could be wrong.
               Recently
an ophthalmologist appraised
the spectacles and saw how fuzzy
and miscolored they made everything
appear.
        He wondered if Cezanne's
whole alphabet of color
erred as a result.
            Call it
Impressionism or call it
a mistake, but Saint-Victoire
seems falsely brown beside
the real thing.
         It's reminiscent
of El Greco, isn't it?
           His portraiture
of Christ and saints and bishops
with their equine faces, upturned
eyes and lengthened bodies
wasn't Gothic, as the critics claim.
El Greco's optic flaw turned
   circles into ovals, ovals
   into candleflames, and horizontals

somehow into verticals.

                              Like Paul
Cezanne he painted what he saw
though all he saw was wrong.
Astigmatism was his problem, not
   perspective.

                      If what resulted
was majestic, how do you explain it?
Does art transcend man's failings?
Do masterpieces simply happen?
Should art historians be qualified
   in ophthalmology?

                        If you regard
such questions as redundant
or ridiculous, then you explain
El Greco.

          You explain Cezanne.

When Life Turns Still

For years I never understood
   why painters painted to compete
   a contradiction.
               If down and up
were opposites by definition,
then stillness and life could not
be more at odds.
             But how
explain away Cezanne,
who posed in absolute perfection
all those apples, grapes, carafes
and cheeses on a tray—one blink
of ripeness just before the rot?
Was every still life for Cezanne
   like music to Stravinsky—not horizontal
   melody but vertical sounds
   in sequence heard in separation,
   each one a song unto itself
   like ranks in a parade?
               Stravinsky's
theory was to make us listen up
instead of listen on.
             And that
made sense.
           If life could end
at any moment, every moment
was eternal and unique.
             Ergo,
Cezanne.
         Ergo, Stravinsky.
Stillness and verticality versus
   motion and protraction . . .
Last night I saw a woman

in her sixties whom I dated
when she turned nineteen.
                              I still
remember how she curled against
my shoulder when we danced—
the scent of lily in her hair,
the oval of her waist.
                          Seeing
how time had made a raisin
of her face, I understood the sacred
once of everything and how
the truthful lies of art
seem truer than our passing lives.
Is it so wrong to show impossibility
   the factual defiance of a dream?
To say what was still is
   because it was?
                        To lead us
grudgingly through silence
into gratitude?
                      Let us
keep still.
                  Let us be grateful.

Winston

"Pink seashells—they easy,
   they in the shallow water,
   but the brown ones, they deep,
   they for the best divers,
   like me, Winston."
                           His gold
   bicuspid glints like a ring
   when he grins.
                      Between us
   gleam shells like armadillos
   or rainbow tornadoes of bone.
"I dive myself for all these
   shell.
                I wash them every one
   myself.
                I dive.
                      I sell.
You want good shell, see Winston."
One size too tight, his shirt
   front screams at the buttonholes.
When he squats, his underwear
   droops through a slit in the seam
   of his shorts scissored from old
   trousers at the knees. . . .
                               I see him
   younger by twenty years,
   a boy after his first dive,
   hawking starfish and grinning ivory.
Then, twenty years ahead,
   too old to dive, toothless,
   selling green sunhats
   woven from belts of palm.

Only that gold biter will not stop
  glistening like wealth itself
  amid this paradise of tourists, orchids,
  shanties and the slopping undertow
  that swills the beach like mop water.

Everything's Important, Everything's Brief

The stroke had killed his English.
All that remained was Swedish
  he no longer spoke because
  the stroke had stilled his tongue
  as well.
          Phoning in his stead
was Monica, who asked if I
would like to hear "the voice
of Tomas."
        A man's voice,
groping for syllables in Swedish
but a man's voice still,
  wobbled over the Atlantic
  to Pittsburgh from Västerås.
               Then,
  perfect and lucid as reveille,
  he played a prelude by Chopin.
Because the stroke had spared
  his limbs, his fingers spoke
  to me for three full minutes
  in Chopin.
        Each note was true
and Baltic as the language in his finest
poems. . . .
        Afterwards, a pause,
followed by blind laughter
in Swedish, then goodbye.
I sat there, phone in hand,
  re-hearing what I'd hear just once
  in all my life.
        He
made me feel . . .
          How can I

say this?
          Imagine something
free and beautiful and captive
all at once—like a finger suddenly
enhanced but still imprisoned by a ring.
Like mercy.
          Like a love so unexpected
that it never left its name.

For Tomas, Who Survived the Axe Blow from Within

The darkening space in my projectile
   lightens with the voice of a great
   poet speaking his Swedish
   poems in English.
                    In fact
   he's speechless, strangled by a stroke
   so that the only voice
   that's his is this one on a tape . . .
I see him blanketed near Stockholm,
   waiting for Monica, thinking
   of midsummer in the archipelago.
If dreams were words, I'd tell
   this man how much I need
   his poems and how true they are.
They heal like sacraments.
                     Instead,
   I watch the road before me
   change into the road behind me
   like a threat faced once and then
   forgotten.
               The poems fill
   the car like Schubert at his best.
They guide me like a compass
   to a home far truer
   than the one I'm heading for.
Which takes more bravery—to live
   with words a poet cannot say
   or steer through Pennsylvania
   darkness in the rain?
                 "His humor
   is wonderful, and we're as close
   as ever."

These words were Monica's
last year, and I repeat them
to the darkness, word by word.
Meanwhile, the tape reverses,
    and I let it spool.
                The compass
steadies to a truer north
than north.
                It says that "patience
is love at rest," and love
means everything.
                Beside such certitude
I seem a man without virtue.

The Horizon at Our Feet

My father said, "Your work
   is never over—always
   one more page."
                         This
from a traveling man whose life
was always one more mile.
I told him that.
                     "Sometimes
I hate the road," he said,
"it's made me so I'm never
happy in one place.
                       Don't
you get started."
                   I never did,
spending my days at universities,
my nights at home.
                 Not
typically the academic, not
totally at home at home,
I think of how I could have lived
and come up blank.
                What's
better than sharing all you know
and all you don't with students
who do just the same?
                 Even
on the worst of days it justifies
the time.
             Or inking out
your real future on white
paper with a fountain pen
and listening to what the writing
teaches you?

Compared to walking
on the moon or curing polio,
it seems so ordinary.
                    And it is.
But isn't living ordinary?
For two and fifty summers
   Shakespeare lived a life
   so ordinary that few scholars
   deal with it.
                    And what of Faulkner
   down in ordinary Oxford, Mississippi?
Or Dickinson, the great recluse?
Or E. B. White, the writer's
   writer?
                    Nothing extraordinary
   there, but, God! what wouldn't
   we give for one more page?

At the Site of the Memorial

1

No soldiers choose to die.
It's what they risk by being
  who and where they are.
It's what they dare while saving
  someone else whose life means
  suddenly as much to them
  as theirs.
          Or more.
                    To honor them
  why speak of duty or the will
  of governments?
               Think first of love
  each time you tell their story.
It gives their sacrifice a name
  and takes from war its glory.

2

Seeing my words in stone
  reminds me of a grave . . .
Not that the words are wrong,
  but seeing them so permanent
  makes me feel posthumous as those
  commemorated here.
              Lawson,
  Gideon, Butler, Pinder,
  Port, Sarnoski, Shughart. . . .
Stephanie Shughart tells me,
  "Randy and I had twenty-two
  months."
            She smiles as if

to prove that gratitude and grief
can be compatible.
                              I want
to believe her . . .
                              Brady, who saved
5,000 men by Medivac
and lived, reads every dead
man's name as if it were
his own.
                    He'll read them in his dreams.
Next to the next of kin,
    I think how all these men
    risked everything for something
    more than living on.
                              Life meant
not one more day for them
but one more act.
                    Just one . . .

The Bodies of Women

Some say they just reflect "the nightly
  love of the sea and the moon."
But life and physiology have never
  rhymed.
            Think of the squat
queen who tranced Marc Antony
and Caesar with her glances to become
all Egypt to them both.
                        Or dancers
who have spines like spears
and walk as if mere walking
were a dance.
            Or nurses in their
white, sure, soft
shoes, nimble as prancers
in motion and just as self-possessed.
Such poise and prowess are the stuff
  of mystery.
            And mystery it is.
What else but mystery imbues
  a woman of stature to subdue
  a mob with nothing but a stance
  or stare?
            Or tells why men
or countrymen can languish
with their goddess gone?
                        Learning
of Piaf's death, Cocteau decided
  not to live.
            For what?
                        For a lifelong
waif whose voice was France
for half a century.

And what
of Om Khalsoum who stilled
the Arab world each time she sang
and drew four million (four
million!) to her funeral?
                    Or Marilyn
Monroe whose public grows
and grows?
                    Is this bewitchery?
Or is it something that will never
   have a name?
                    Or does it simply
mean that women live within
their bodies to the end—and past
the end?
                    Not so for men
who seem to leave their bodies
as they age, regarding what was once
an instrument as now a thing
of no or little use.
                    For those
whose destination is themselves,
what are such losses but a nuisance,
not a destiny?
                    Compared to love
or happiness or children, they appear
at best as vanities.
                    See
for yourselves.
                    The eyes of any
woman say it takes more bravery
to be and bear than to beget.
Or finally just *be*, with no
   defenses, no illusions, no regrets.

Once Upon a Wedding

Watching two lives converge
   through all your predecessors down
   the centuries to you is miracle
   enough.
            But all that is
is history.
              You're more than that.
If choosing is the most that freedom
   means, you're free.
              If choosing
   one you love for life
   is freedom at its best,
   you're at your best today.
No wonder we're exuberant.
Today's become an instant
   anniversary for all of us.
You've brought us back to what's
   the most important choice
   of all.
          You've shown that where
   we come from matters less
   than who we are, and who
   we are is what we choose
   to be . . .
          We're all familiar
   with the risks.
             No matter how
   or whom we love, we know
   we're each on loan to one
   another for a time.
             We know
   we're God's employees picked
   for unforeseen assignments

we'll be given on the way.
                        The secret
is to love until the summoning,
regardless of the odds . . .
                        Go now
together in the unison of mates.
Go happily with all our hopes
  and all our blessings.
                        And with God's.

For Sam and Dawn

The Holy Surprise of Right Now

If you can see your path laid out ahead of you step
by step, then you know it's not your path.
—Joseph Campbell

Inside Brooks Brothers' windows
   it's July.
               Sport shirts on sleek
dummies speak in turquoise,
polo, Bermuda and golf.
Outside, it's very much the first
   of March.
               The sport shirts say
today's tomorrow and the present
tense be damned.
               They tell me
to forget that here's the only place
we have.
               They claim what matters
most is never now but next.
I've heard this argument before.
It leaves me sentenced to the future,
   and that's much worse than being
   sentenced to the past.
               The past
at least was real just once . . .
               What's
called religion offers me the same.
Life's never what we have
   but what's to come.
               But where
did Christ give heaven its address
except within each one of us?
So, anyone who claims it's not

within but still ahead is contradicting
God.
   But why go on?
I'm sick of learning to anticipate.
I never want to live a second
 or a season or a heaven in advance
 of when I am and where.
I need the salt and pepper
 of uncertainty to know I'm still
 alive.
   It makes me hunger
 for the feast I call today.
It lets desire keep what
 satisfaction ends.
     Lovers
remember that the way that smoke
remembers fire.
    Between anticipation
and the aggravation of suspense, I choose
suspense.
   I choose desire.

Ahead of Time

Her letter, mailed from Saranac,
  is dated 1926.
                My mother's
writing to my aunt.
                It's two
years since she told her father,
"Dad, I'm marrying Sam
and not the man you had
in mind."
                That's decades more
  than half a century ago.
My mother and my aunt are dead.
I'm well past sixty when I share
  my mother's letter with my wife.
It stills us like a resurrection.
Later I read it to my son
  and to his wife.
                They tell me
how alive it seems as if
a woman neither ever knew
is speaking in this very room
to each of us.
                The letter's full
of questions I can answer,
  but the time for answering is over.
I realize my life's already longer
  than my mother's was by almost
  thirty years.
                The letter in my hand
  is older than the two of us.
The more I read, the less
  there is to read until
  I reach the bottom of the page.

The last sentence ends
with a hyphen.
There's no page two.

Ballad of the Jolly Broker

Nothing was surer amid all the furor
than watching a stock that I picked on a hunch
make rich men of paupers, and paupers of fools,
and all in the pinch that it took to eat lunch.

My betting and cheering took real engineering.
I guessed and I gauged and I bet and I prayed
from the dawn of the bull to the dusk of the bear
where fortunes were waiting and fortunes were made.

The world of percents is a world that resents
whenever its buyouts are less than a steal.
Its language is numbers, and numbers are lethal,
and all that makes sense is the luck of the deal.

You have to like poker to be a good broker.
You have to take chances and hope for the best.
Buy cheap and sell dear is the law of the market,
and woe unto those who forget or protest.

Like any good broker I loved to play poker,
but poker's a gamble where all that you've got
is the lure of the cards and the stack of the chips
and the dice of the deal and the pay of the pot . . .

I took all my winnings that some called my sinnings,
and lived like a king where the snow never fell.
I drank all my juices and swallowed my pills,
and bet on the races, and down came hell . . .

It cost me my wife in the prime of my life.
It made me content with much less than the best.

I worked for the day when I never would work,
and the money was sure, and the honey was rest.

If you'd rather be healthy than feeble and wealthy . . .
If you'd rather be happy than wed to a bed,
then think of a man with a millionaire's tan
who died half a lifetime before he was dead.

September 11, 2001

1

The hawk seems almost napping
  in his glide.
             His arcs are perfect
as geometry.
             His eyes hunger
for something about to panic,
  something small and unaware.
Higher by two thousand feet
  an airbus vectors for its port,
  its winglights aiming dead
ahead like eyesight.
             The natural
and scheduled worlds keep happening
according to their rules . . .
             "We interrupt
this program . . ."
             Inch by inch
the interruption overrules both worlds,
engulfing us like dustfall
from a building in collapse.
             The day
turns dark as an eclipse.
             We head
for home as if to be assured
that home is where we left it.

2

Before both towers drowned
  in their own dust, someone
  downfloated from the hundredth floor.

Then there were others—plunging,
   stepping off or diving in tandem,
   hand in hand, as if the sea
   or nets awaited them.
                     "My God,
   people are jumping!"
                 Of all
   the thousands there, we saw
   those few, just those, freefalling
   through the sky like flotsam from a blaze . . .
Nightmares of impact crushed us.
We slept like the doomed or drowned,
   then woke to oratory , vigils,
   valor, journalists declaring war
   and, snapping from aerials or poles,
   the furious clamor of flags.

Ballad of a Returnee

He knew he was older and taller.
He saw that the towns were the same.
What made them seem suddenly smaller?
What made him feel somehow to blame

for all that was done to a village
to save a surrounded platoon?
The huts were just booty to pillage
on a hillscape as spare as the moon.

A man with one leg saw him walking
and offered him tea on a mat.
They spent the whole afternoon talking
while his wife cooked the head of a cat.

It wasn't his squad he remembered.
It wasn't the sergeant at Hue
who found his lieutenant dismembered
and buried him there where he lay.

What troubled him most were the places
that once were just places to fight.
He thought of the nightfighters' faces
all blackened to blend with the night.

The whores in their teens were forgotten
and gone were their overnight dates,
and grown were the idly begotten
whose fathers were back in the States.

He never regretted returning.
At least he had lessened his dread.

But the toll that it took for the learning
was 58,000 dead.

He walked in a daze near the water.
He sat all alone on the shore
like a man making peace with the slaughter,
though the price for this peace was war.

Dining with Montaigne

What's welcome is your French disdain
  of dogma.
                 Quotations from Solon,
Horace, Virgil, and Plato,
  of course . . .
                Digressions on food,
ambition and fatherhood, assuredly . . .
But all in the spirit of conversation—
  without an angle, so to speak.
When you call marriage a "discreet
  and conscientious voluptuousness,"
  I partially agree.
              After
  you explain that "valor" and "value"
  are etymologically akin, I see
  the connection.
              Nothing seems
contentious.
             Your views on cruelty
  recall Tertullian's platitude
  that men fear torture more than death.
Of honors you are tolerant, noting
  that honors are most esteemed
  when rare and quoting Martial
  in support: "To him who thinks
  none bad, whoever can seem good?"
If mere consistency identifies
  small minds, you never were small.
One incident explains: perpetuating
  family names you called a vanity,
  and yet you willed your name
  and fortune to your daughter's
  youngest son.

Since she was married
twice and had two families,
two hundred years of litigation
followed.
Why?
Because
Montaigne the *grand-père* silenced
Montaigne the philosopher, which proves
once more that irony, not reason,
rules the blood.
Otherwise,
your breadth of thought amazes me.
Each meal's a feast whose menu
is the universe.
So here's a toast,
my friend, across four centuries.
To essays that seem to write
themselves and sound like tabletalk.
To hospitality of mind where nothing
is immune from scrutiny.
To all
that leaves me wisely confused
but even in confusion, wiser.

Facing the Lake with St.-Ex

A dozen mallards squawk
  in a shortarm vee above
  Lake Huron.
              Without a physicist
  among them, they slip each other's
  jetwash and wing northward
  equidistantly at cloud-speed.
I put aside the wartime prose
  of Antoine de St.-Exupery
  and track the ducks to Canada.
To be dull as a duck aground
  but awesome in flight and even
  more awesome in print describes
  St.-Ex in life and death.
If poetry is prose that soars,
  his prose in fact is poetry.
It made Consuelo overlook
  his dalliances, his sleight-of-hand
  with cards, his sudden absences.
How many men dare gravity
  with wings and words and win
  as no one did before
  or since or ever?
              Meanwhile,
  over the rhythm of waves
  the mallards are rowing the wind
  in perfect rhyme to show
  what's possible without instruction.

Breakdown

Like soldiers ordered to "Fall in,"
  platoons of starlings swoop
  and muster on a telephone line.
Equidistant and at birds' attention,
  they mimic ranks at "Parade Rest."
Suddenly they dive into the air
  on cue, swirling in a bluster
  of wings like a dream gone mad.
For just that long, I think
  that madness rules the world,
  despite appearances.
                   "Change
  the rhythm," Pindar predicted,
  "and the walls of the city will fall."
It takes so little . . .
             Vary
  the height and width of any step
  by just a fraction, and the rhythm
  of a stairway dies.
             Change
  traffic patterns, and we slacken
  to the speed of doubt.
             Or let
come war, and we're undone
as if the sea breathed in
and never out against our shores,
surrounding, pounding, drowning
everything.
             It imitates what happens
when I'm writing, and the words
won't perch.
             They swirl confused
as any flock in flight.

They're swirling
now.
        I'm losing touch
with what I should be saying,
and I can't remember what I think
I meant.
        The tempo's gone
completely . . .
        Pindar was right.

Thus Spake Mercutio

Be they belaureled as the king
    of cats, I'll not recant.
Euphues is no more poet
    than a pig, oinking his drivel
    at the moon.
                        And singsong rhymers
    by the millions shrink to nil
    beside the singer of the "Song
    of Songs."
                        Nor does allegiance
    to a master-piper matter
    in the least.
                        Name one of all
    the acolytes who formed the Tribe
    of Ben.
                        Lovers of a sort
    may toast the aromatic meat
    of wenches, but their rhapsodies
    at midnight disappear by dawn.
And those who pen for pelf
    and hawk their words as marketeers
    deserve the wages of disdain.
The time of breath is much
    too brief for humbug.
                        Let us
    have poetry that strikes us dumb
    or leaves us stabbed so deeply
    that the wound in perpetuity stays raw.
Let us have that or nothing.

Arms and the Word

Great sailors though they were,
  the Greeks abhorred the sea.
What was it but a gray
  monotony of waves, wetness
  in depth, an element by nature
  voyager-unfriendly and capricious?
Sailing in sight of shore,
  they always beached at night
  to sleep before the next day's
  rowing.
        Taming the sea
  by beating it with rods
  they named the ultimate insanity—
  a metaphor too obvious to paraphrase.
In short, they knew a widow-
  maker when they saw one.
            Still,
  for honor, commerce, or a kidnapped
  queen, they waged their lives
  against what Homer called wine-dark
  and deep.
        Some came back never.
Some learned too late that pacing
  a deck was far less hazardous
  than facing what awaited them
  at home . . .
        Homer would praise
  their iliads and odysseys in song.
Aeschylus, Euripides, and Sophocles
  would watch and wait, then write
  of wars much closer to the heart.
They knew the lives of men—
  no matter how adventurous—

would end as comedies or tragedies.
They wrote that both were fundamentally
    and finally domestic.
                        Homer
    could sing his fill.
                        The dramatists
    dared otherwise.
                        Compared
    to troubles in a family, they saw
    this business with the sea and swords—
    regardless of the risk—as minor.

PART FOUR

Ongoing Presences Have No Past Tense

Just Words

In Arabic a single word
 describes the very act
 of taking a position.
                    Greeks
pronounce three syllables
to signify the sense of doom
that all Greeks fear when things
are going very well.
                    As for
the shameful ease we feel
when bad news happens
to someone else, including
friends?
           In Greek—one word.
To designate the hose that funnels
 liquid fire down the turret
 of a tank in battle, the Germans
speak one word.
                    It's three
lines long but still one word.
And as for John, Matthew,
 Mark and Luke?
                    There's not
a surname in the lot.
                    With just
one name they match in memory
the immortality of martyrs.
                    The longer
they're dead, the more they live. . . .
I praise whatever mates
 perception with precision!
                    It asks
us only to be spare and make

the most of least.
                    It simplifies
and lets each word sound final
as a car door being shut
but perfect as a telegram to God.

Casanova to God

I thought of women basically
  as fruit: delectable when ripe,
  dismissible past prime,
  disposable when old.
                    I'm not
to blame.
            You made young women
irresistible, not I.
                My sin—
if it was sin at all—was ultimate
enjoyment of Your handiwork.
That girl from Padua—the supple
  once-ness of her kiss . . .
                  Her cousin
from Trieste—the way her breasts
announced themselves . . .
                Surely
You appreciate the patience and the skill
it takes to bring a virgin
to the point where shame means nothing.
I'm not a rapist, after all.
The ones I chose were single,
  willing, totally agreeable.
They wanted to be loved deliciously.
Not roughly like those toughs who pinched
  them in the street, but step
  by gentle step and never in a hurry.
First, some conversation.
               Then,
  a kiss on either cheek.
Then everything that You alone
  could see: a jettison of clothes,
  my palm along her inner thigh,

our loins in juncture as we hugged,
the mounting puffs and shudders
on the sheets, the parting, the repose.
It made me marvel at the way
  You fashioned us for mating
  face to face—essentially
  two kinds of kissing happening
  in one position all at once.
Because I reached perfection in the act,
  some called me a philanderer . . .
Pronounce me guilty if You like . . .
I'm reconciled.
                    I did what I
  alone could do when I could
  do it.
                Who says desire dies?
Today I'm tended by a nurse
  who spoons me noodles from a cup.
She tells me to relax.
                    Relax?
When a woman naked underneath
  her uniform is but a breath
  away from Giacomo Girolamo
  Casanova of Venice?
                    Impossible.

A Toast for the Likes of Two

Who was it wrote, "If women
   had mustaches, they would somehow
   make them beautiful.
                              Look
   what they've done with breasts!"
Who disagrees?
                         Doesn't the Bible
   say a woman just an inch
   from death will keep an eye
   for color?
                    And don't philosophers
   assert that women sacrifice
   the ultimate on beauty's altar?
And love's?
                    Why scoff at that?
Are the male gods of money,
   fame, and power more deserving?
What's money but guilt?
                                   What's fame
   but knowing people you will never
   know will know your name?
What's power but pride translated
   into force?
                    Are these worth more
   than what sustains us to the end?
Consider Bertha.
                    Eighty, blind
   and diabetic, she believed that death's
   real name was Harold.
                              "I want
   to know what Harold has to offer,"
   she would say.

She'd seen
her children's children's children
and presumed she had a poet's right
to give a name to death, if so
she chose.
Chuckling to herself,
she rocked and waited for this last
adventure in her life . . .
Then
there was Jane, who mothered seven
and left unfinished all her art
by choice as if to prove
that incompleteness is the rule
of life where nothing ends
the way it should . . . or when.
Two weeks before her funeral
she called all seven to her bed
to say, "I hope to see you all
again . . . but not right away . . ."
So here's to the honor of Bertha,
and here's to the glory of Jane!
Let them be spoken of wherever
beauty's lovers gather to applaud
the beauty of love.
Let them
not rest in peace but thrive
in everlasting action, doing
what they love the most.
Who wants
a heaven that's equivalent to one
long sleep?
Those crypted, supine
saints in their basilicas can keep
the dream of their Jerusalem.

                    The soul
   was meant for more than that.
Pray for us, St. Bertha.
Pray for us, St. Jane.

Looking into a Tulip

Have you ever looked into a flower, Mr. Gable?
—Grace Kelly

Look in, and the flower stares back.
Its iris offers you the very
  whites, blues, pinks
  and lavenders of God.
                 Each petal
  revels in the final glory
  of itself.
        For those distracted
 by horizons I propose five minutes
in the company of tulips.
              One
  tulip will suffice in all
  its purple understatement.
              Look deep
  and see what's primping to its prime
  before it fades and falls,
  and you'll be mesmerized for life.
Brides in their wedding veils
  would understand.
         They know
  it's not duration but expression
  that survives our days.
          They flower
  in their one-time gowns
  just once for just one day.
Even though it ends, it stays.

After Arlington

It lasts like a parade in place
   with only the essentials cut
   in rhyming white headstones:
   last names, initials,
   rank, branches of service.
The names answer up in a muster
   of silence while Washington's a-glut
   with traffic, vectoring jets
   and disproportion.
                 Maple groves,
   road signs and gardens
   remember Lady Bird and LBJ.
Facing the Department of Commerce,
   Reagan's billion-dollar
   palace rivals in square
   feet the whole damn Pentagon.
Roosevelt's granite marker,
   scaled as he asked to the length
   and width of his desk, is harder
   to find.
              Jack Kennedy,
   his widow, two children,
   and his brothers share one plot.
Across the slow Potomac,
   the names in black marble
   of 58,000 futile deaths
   consecrate less than an acre.

Ballad of the One-Legged Marine

My left leg was gone with the boot still on—
the boot that I laced in the morning.
I felt like a boy who had stepped on a toy
and made it explode without warning.

They choppered me back to a medical shack
with no one but corpsmen to heed me.
I stared at the sky and prayed I would die,
and I cursed when the nurse came to feed me.

I knew that I must, so I tried to adjust
while orderlies struggled to teach me
the will of the crutch and the skill of the cane
and assured me their methods would reach me.

The President came with his generals tame
and explained why he never relieved us.
But the red, white, and blue of my lone, right shoe
told the world how he lied and deceived us.

They buried my shin and my bones and my skin
an ocean away from this writing.
But pain finds a way on each given day
to take me straight back to the fighting

when I served with the Corps in a slaughterhouse war
where we tallied our killings like cattle,
as if these explain why the armies of Cain
behave as they do in a battle . . .

Whatever's a bore, you can learn to ignore,
but a leg's not a limb you like leaving.

So you deal with regret and attempt to forget
what always is there for the grieving.

If you look for a clue while I stand in a queue,
you can't tell what's real from prosthetic.
I walk with a dip that begins at my hip,
but I keep it discreet and aesthetic.

If you're ordered on line and step on a mine,
you learn what it means to be only
a name on a chart with a hook in your heart
and a life that turns suddenly lonely.

Lose arms, and you're left incomplete and bereft.
Lose legs, and you're fit for a litter.
Lose one at the knee, and you're just like me
with night after night to be bitter.

For Ray Fagan

A Time of No Shadows

Immortality?
     Too general a concept.
Some say it's never-ending time,
 which means it's long on myth
 and short on meaning.
       Some say
 it's never to be known until
 it's ours.
     Some say, some say . . .
I stand with those who think
 it could be quick as any instant
 going on and on and on
 within itself like poetry or music
 or a kiss.
     That comes as close
 as anything to God's, "I am
Who am."
     No past.
       No memory.
No future but the time at hand
 that's passing even as it's born . . .
Once I was driving due southeast
 through Pennsylvania.
       Highways
 were broad and dangerous and everyone's.
As I ran out of Pennsylvania,
 farm by farm, I noticed
 border signs that welcomed me
 to Maryland where Rand McNally
 said that Maryland began.
I knew the earth was still
 the earth in Maryland or Pennsylvania.

I knew I stayed the same,
   border or no border . . .
                   From here
into hereafter could be just
like that—our selfsame selves
translated instantly from state
to state to God alone
knows what. . . .
              That's immortality.

Ongoing Presences Have No Past Tense

I keep whatever stays as intimate
   as breath and, like all breathing,
   of the instant: my father's aftershave,
   the whiteness of his shirts, his hair
   still black at eighty-two,
   the hats he always wore brim up,
   the eyes of Cynthia gone sullen
   with desire, supper in Geneva
   when a waiter in tuxedo boned
   the lemon sole as deftly as a surgeon
   operating on an eye, the day
   of Kennedy's murder when all
   the clocks struck nil and stayed there,
   my last goodbye to Jane
   and how we sensed it as we spoke.
Compared to these, who cares
   if Candidate Twice and Candidate Once
   insult the day with presidential
   dreams?
          For them today's
a preface, nothing more.
               The same
holds true for all who bet
on dynasties, prognostications, jackpots,
or the gold of fools.
            I trust
the body's unforgettable assurances
that know what's true without
discussion or hypocrisy.
            The teeth
with just one bite can tell
an apple from a pear.

                    The tongue
can savor at a touch what's salt,
what's sugar.
                    Balsam and skunk
cannot confuse the nose.
Even in darkness the hand
  knows silk from gabardine.
Whatever makes a sound and what
  resounds when sound evaporates
  is music to the ear.
                    The eye
does not discriminate, and everything
in its complete democracy is ours
in perpetuity to keep as near
as here and dearer than now.

Notre Dame du Lac

1

Everywhere the same campus trees—
   fifty autumns thicker, taller
   and scheduled to sleeve their naked
   bark in January's ermine.
A male and female cardinal
   peck at huckleberries on a limb.
Paired for life, they beak
   each berry as their last and first.
Sparrows cling to branches,
   wires, sheer brick walls,
   anything where they can roost.
A chipmunk scoots and pauses
   by the numbers.
               Unlike all peacock
   prancers on parade or the zombie
   stomp of soldiery, backpacking
   students cycle, rollerblade
   and stroll to their different drummers.
They pass like Giacometti's
   striders—eyes full front
   but aimed at destinations still
   within themselves. . . .
               Beyond
   Nantucket a jet's about to crash.
Bradley's challenging Gore.
Ted Hesburgh's fit and eighty-two
   with one good eye.
             "May I
   serve God better with one eye
   than I did with two."
             Seated

behind me at a football game,
a woman from Dallas tells me
her Pittsburgh mother had an uncle—
Leo O'Donnell, a doctor.
                                    She knows
I've flown from Pittsburgh for the day.
Eighty thousand cheer around us.
"O'Donnell," she repeats.
                                    I swallow
and say that Dr. O'Donnell funded
"my scholarship to study here"
a half-century ago.
                                    The odds
are eighty thousand plus to one
that I should meet his Texas niece
today in this crammed stadium
in Indiana, but I do.
                                    What else
is there to say?
                         It's now
all over the world.
                                    Everything's
happening.
                         Anything can happen.

         2

We've journeyed back to grass
   and souvenirs and beige bricks.
The sky's exactly the same.
Acre by acre, the campus
   widens like a stage designed
   for a new play.
                         Why
do we gawk like foreigners

at residence halls no longer
ours but somehow ours
in perpetuity?
                    We visit them
like their alumni—older
but unchanged.
                    Half a century
of students intervenes.
                         They stroll
among us now, invisible
but present as the air before
they fade and disappear.
                         It's like
the day we swam St. Joseph's
Lake.
          We churned the surface
into suds with every stroke and kick.
After we crossed, the water
    stilled and settled to a sheen
    as if we never swam at all.
One memory was all we kept
    to prove we'd been together
    in that very lake, and swimming.
Each time we tell this story,
    someone says we're living out
    a dream.
                    We say we're only
reuniting with the lives
we lived.
               As long as we
can say they were, they *were* . . .
And what they were, we are.

National Prayer Breakfast

Conventioneers from thirty-seven
  countries throng the banquet
  hall to hear the message.
A clergyman tells God to bless
  the fruit and rolls.
                    The President
speaks up for Reagan, Martin
Luther King, and having faith
in faith.
            Love is the common
theme, most of it touching,
all of it frank, unburdening
and lengthy.
               If faith is saying so,
then this is faith.
                The problem is
that I must be the problem.
I've always thought that faith
  declaimed too publicly destroys
  the mystery.
             Years back,
when Brother Antoninus yelled
at listeners to hear the voice
of Jesus in them, Maura whispered,
"The Jesus in me doesn't talk
that way."
            Later, when I saw
a placard bannering, "Honk,
if you love Jesus," I thought
of Maura's words and passed
in silence . . .
            Jesus in fact
spoke Aramaic in Jerusalem,

foretold uninterrupted life
and sealed it with a resurrection.
If He asked me to honk
   in praise of that, I'd honk
   all day.
            But rising from the dead
for me seems honk enough
since no one's done it since,
and no one did it earlier or ever.
Others might disagree, and that's
   their right.
            But there's an inner
voice I hear that's one
on one and never out of date.
It's strongest when it's most subdued.
I'll take my Jesus straight.

The More We Know, the Less We Feel Until

Down from her waist, she rolled
  her white bikini bottom
  like a wee inverted sock.
Sunned evenly from chin to shin,
  she walked and twirled the bottom
  like a shoelace to her car.
To gawk behind a naked
  girl's behind in St. Tropez
  is not unusual.
              In fact,
  it's almost trite.
              But this
was different.
           Her walking asked
what form's more beautiful
in all of nature than the female
body in motion?
           It spoke
like modern Paris architecture,
  giving not a damn for my approval
  or dissent, but being absolutely
  what it is, take it or leave it . . .
Secure within the splendor
  of herself, she scarcely noticed me.
Of, if she did, she relegated me
  to that dull tribe who wear,
  like public transportation passengers,
  the same church-face
  from breath to death.
           Her face
was every oiled inch of her
from eyebrows beachward
to her toes.

All this she bared
as shamelessly as any wife
undressing as her husband watched.
It woke me up.
                    The south
of France became the *Cote
d'Azur.*
                    The beach was not
a shore of stones but suddenly
the Riviera.
                    The sky
demanded to be memorized.
The wind remembered it should be
    the wind, and every breath
    it billowed softly from the sea
    was mine to swallow like a song.

Mustangs

5th Special Basic Class, U. S. Marine Corps

Older by fifty years,
  we grouped for photographs beside
  apartment BOQs that once
  were Quonset huts.
               The new
lieutenants held us in embarrassing
esteem.
          Of some three hundred
in our old battalion, three
were killed in combat, and the rest
lived on to die of the usual
or simply to survive and re-unite.
Necklaced with tags to prove
  we were who we were, we met
  without bravado.
             Grandfathers mostly,
we drank black coffee like alumni
and avoided politics.
            Two days
together placed us squarely
in our generation.
           No one pretended
to be other than himself.
            We parted
as we parted half a century
before, uncertain when or where
we'd meet again.
          Or if.

In the Time of the Tumult of Nations

We thought that the worst was behind us
 in the time of the tumult of nations.
We planned and we saved for the future
 in the time of the tumult of nations.
The crowds in the streets were uneasy
 in the time of the tumult of nations.
We murdered our annual victims
 in the time of the tumult of nations.
We were fined if we smoked in the cities
 in the time of the tumult of nations.
We gave and deducted our givings
 in the time of the tumult of nations.
We kept the bad news from the children
 in the time of the tumult of nations.
We wakened from nightmares with headaches
 in the time of the tumult of nations.
We voted for men we distrusted
 in the time, in the time, in the time,
 in the time of the tumult of nations.

In the time of the tumult of nations
 the ones who were wrong were the loudest.
In the time of the tumult of nations
 the poets were thought to be crazy.
In the time of the tumult of nations
 the President answered no questions.
In the time of the tumult of nations
 protesters were treated like traitors.
In the time of the tumult of nations
 the airports were guarded by soldiers.
In the time of the tumult of nations
 young women kept mace in their purses.
In the time of the tumult of nations

the rich were exempt in their mansions.
In the time of the tumult of nations
    we waited for trouble to happen.
In the time of the tumult of nations
    we lived for the weekends like children.

Like children we clung to our playthings
    in the time of the tumult of nations.
We huddled in burglar-proof houses
    in the time of the tumult of nations.
We said that the poor had it coming
    in the time of the tumult of nations.
We readied our handguns for trouble
    in the time of the tumult of nations.
We tuned in to war every evening
    in the time of the tumult of nations.
We watched as the bombs burned the cities
    in the time of the tumult of nations.
The name of the game was destruction
    in the time of the tumult of nations.
We knew we were once better people
    in the time of the tumult of nations.
We pretend we are still the same people
    in the time, in the time, in the time,
    in the time of the tumult of nations.

For Which It Stands

Crosswinds have slashed the flag
  so that the thirteenth ribbon
  dangles free or coils around
  the flagpole like a stripe.
                     What's left
keeps fluttering in red-and-white
defiance.
           Somehow the tattering
seems apropos.
              The President
proclaims we'll be at war forever—
not war for peace but war
upon war, though hopefully not here.
Believers in eternal re-election
  hear his pitch and pay.
                 In Washington,
God's lawyer turns pianist
and sings a hymn he wrote
himself.
         Elsewhere, California's
governor believes in California's
governor, and football bowls
are named for Mastercard, Pacific
Life, Con-Agra, and Tostitos.
Out west a plan to gerrymander
  Colorado (Texas-style) fails,
  but barely.
         Asked why no flag
is studded in his coat lapel
or decorates his aerial, a veteran
responds, "I wear my flag
on my heart—I don't wear
my heart on my sleeve."

Today
for once we're spared the names
of occupying soldiers shot
or rocketed to fragments in Iraq.
Collateral damage?
                    Two boys,
their mother, and both grandparents.
No names for them . . .
                    Just Arabs.

A Czech Susannah in Cannes

Supinely tanning at attention
  on her towel, Lefka's beyond
  description.
        The naked breasts
  of lounging women often lounge
  themselves, their shapes re-shaping
  differently with every turn.
Not Lefka's.
        Mounding and barely
  pendant, they're peepingly awake.
They match in sepia her swimmer's
  thighs, her sprinter's ankles
  and her navel-centered midriff
  diving to the loins where gold
  triangular lamé protects
  the first and last of privacies.
Her face is all of her
  from eyebrows down to insteps.
Simply by being, she tells us
  that desire's not the same as passion,
  passion but the energy of love,
  and love the silence after ecstasy
  when ecstasy has come and gone.
Like any orchid in its prime,
  she's there to be observed and memorized,
  and so we ogle like the elders.
Watching, we become bewitched.
The more we watch, the more
  we share with France "an enviable
  ease with pleasure."
        Unease
  awaits us, and we know that in advance.
But now who cares?

                        The sun's
noon-high.
                        The sea seems placid
as a pool.
                        And nothing in the sky's
unclouded distance can distract us
from a girl so beautiful she makes
our daily dread of suffering
or violent death seem suddenly
the stuff of fantasy, not fact.

Towels

What purpose have they but to rub
  skin dry by being drawn behind
  the back two-handed down
  the showered spine or fluffed
  between the thighs and elsewhere?
Yardgoods lack what towels
  proffer in sheer, plump tuft.
Wadded after use and flung
  in hampers to be washed, they clump
  like the tired laundry of men
  who sweat for a living.
                              Spun dry
  or spreadeagled to the sun,
  they teach us what renewal means.
Touch them when they're stacked or racked,
  and what you're touching is abundance
  in waiting.
                    Imprinted with the names
  of Hilton or the Ritz, they daub
  with equal deft the brows
  of bandits or the breasts of queens.
What else did Pilate reach for
  when he washed his hands of Christ
  before the multitudes?
                              Even
  when retired to the afterlife of rags,
  they still can buff the grills
  of Chryslers, Fallingwater's windows
  or important shoes.
                          However
  small, it seems they have
  their part to play.

But then,
en route from use to uselessness,
it's no small asset ever
to be always good at something.

Mediterranean Update

Whatever let it be a pleasure
   made it end like anything
   that dies before we think
   it should.
            The aisles of lavender,
   the sea "between the land,"
   the houses cut from rock
   where Yeats lived last, the yachts
   moored hull to hull at anchor,
   and the wind from Africa that's known
   as the *libeccio* all blurred
   like painter's pigments fractioned
   into bits.
           "Everything's the same
   but us," I said, "because
   we've come back once too often."
French television flashed
   a raid by F-16s in Gaza
   followed by a sacrificial bombing
   in Jerusalem.
           The detonated bodies
   sprawled alike.
           "Same intent,"
I said, "but different weapons."
The prospect made me kick
   aside a core of cardboard
   from a toilet paper roll
   discarded near a dumpster.
           Later
   we indulged ourselves in sun
   and surf—our way of fiddling
   while tomorrow burned.

                    Romeos
roamed the beaches, sporting
their scrotal pouches.
                    Women
wore nil but thongs and pubic
patches.
            So many thronged
the waves I thought of mullets
or ale-wives surging in frenzy. . . .
Three hours east by air,
    oppressor and oppressed were being
    filmed in battles we would watch
    while dining later in Antibes
    or sipping cappuccino by the pool.

Seesaws

The bigger the tomb, the smaller the man.
The weaker the case, the thicker the brief.
The deeper the pain, the older the wound.
The graver the loss, the dryer the tears.

The truer the shot, the slower the aim.
The quicker the kiss, the sweeter the taste.
The viler the crime, the vaguer the guilt.
The louder the price, the cheaper the ring.

The higher the climb, the sheerer the slide.
The steeper the odds, the shrewder the bet.
The rarer the chance, the brasher the risk.
The colder the snow, the greener the spring.

The braver the bull, the wiser the cape.
The shorter the joke, the surer the laugh.
The sadder the tale, the dearer the joy.
The longer the life, the briefer the years.

The Necessary Brevity of Pleasures

Prolonged, they slacken into pain
  or sadness in accordance with the law
  of apples.
              One apple satisfies.
Two apples cloy.
              Three apples
  glut.
      Call it a tug-of-war
between enough and more
than enough, between sufficiency
and greed, between the stay-at-homers
and globe-trotting see-the-worlders.
Like lovers seeking heaven in excess,
  the hopelessly insatiable forget
  how passion sharpens appetites
  that gross indulgence numbs.
Result?
      The haves have not
what all the have-nots have
since much of having is the need
to have.
      Even my dog
knows that—and more than that.
He slumbers in a moon of sunlight,
  scratches his twitches and itches
  in measure, savors every bite
  of grub with equal gratitude
  and stays determinedly in place
  unless what's suddenly exciting
  happens.
      Viewing mere change
as threatening, he relishes a few
undoubtable and proven pleasures

to enjoy each day in sequence
and with canine moderation.
They're there for him in waiting,
and he never wears them out.

Parting Shot

Nothing symphonic will come of this,
  nothing of consequence, and nothing
  to silence those whose business
  is creating funerals where widows
  in their twenties carry folded flags
  to empty bedrooms.
                    Pronouncers
and announcers govern from their desks
  while corporals and captains pay
  the price in loss.
              I cite
the history of Danielle Green.
She basketballed her way from poverty
  to Notre Dame, played guard
  with champions and honed a shot
  she took lefthanded just beyond
  the paint and rarely missed.
Later in Iraq a bomb
  exploded near enough to claim
  her shooting hand.
                 Others
lost more, and many lost
  everything that anyone can lose.
Some say that poetry has other
  themes to sing about than that.
If that's the case, what good
  is poetry that shies away from pain
  and amputation?
            What else can make us
feel, not merely know, that severed
  limbs and lives can never
  be replaced?
            And all for what?

For the Time Being

A day will come when nothing
　　will matter but the day itself.
No one will care if what's
　　predicted in the *Farmers' Almanac*
　　comes true or not—or fret
　　with crossword puzzles just
　　to pass the time—or ask
　　why total frankness is acceptable
　　in surgery or love or art
　　but otherwise considered shameful.
A day will come when even
　　the best will not be good
　　enough.
　　　　　　　What's seen as quality
　　will crumble under scrutiny.
Total frauds will speak as saints
　　while torturers receive the Eucharist
　　at solemn Masses and be blessed.
When salt exceeds the price
　　of silver, banks will close.
Drivers will spend a month's
　　wages for a tank of gas.
Armies will be staffed by foreigners.
Doctors will be paid in promises.
Gravesites will be taxed as real estate
　　and levied on the next of kin.
A day will come when no one
　　will remember who we were
　　or where we lived or how.
Headlines will exaggerate the trivial
　　to make the unimportant seem
　　important.

History will vary
with historians until the past
recedes and disappears like snow.
False prophets will foretell the worst
and be believed because the dreams
of liars are immune to contradiction.
The world will change from what
it was to what it is although
the earth will keep repeating
its ballet in orbit to remind us
every morning that today's that day.

The Real Wager

The cause of all human misery: the inability
to sit contentedly alone in a room.
—Blaise Pascal

Monsieur Pascal, I'm sitting here
   alone in Scranton, Pennsylvania.
Radisson has rented me this room
   with no amenities but lotion,
   towels, bathsoap, and a sewing kit.
My family's three hundred miles
   west by southwest.
                         To be frank,
   I'm not content.
                         Though Robert
   Louis Stevenson could say
   intelligent men, delayed
   in railroad waiting rooms
   for days without a book, should not
   be bored, I'm bored.
                         Despite
   three books I've brought along
   in case, I'm bored to my toenails.
That puts me on the side
   of human misery and culpable
   stupidity, I guess.
                         But what
   of those who face the bookless
   loneliness of solitary confinement?
Both you and Mister Stevenson
   might say they should be most
   content, but men have lost
   their minds or brained themselves
   against a wall in such conditions.

Granted, there are exceptions.
Aleksandr Solzhenitsyn scrawled
    The Gulag Archipelago on toilet
    paper in Siberia.
                    And prisoners
    of war have stubbornly survived
    cold years of total isolation.
Excepting the exceptions, you
    and Mr. Stevenson make sense
    but only if our times of solitude
    or long delays conclude.
                    After all,
    the art of making time irrelevant
    by just abandoning ourselves
    to life the way that swimmers
    float and let the ocean be
    their beds is something everyone
    should learn.
                    However, the ocean
    must stay calm just as the room
    you specify must not be locked,
    and Stevenson's late train arrive
    at last.
                If not, we're talking
    human misery as unrelieved
    as pain itself—we're talking hell.

Caesarean

And the Guernsey lowing in its stanchion,
   waiting to be milked, blood
   on the udders, and the farmer grim
   and saying she is only good
   for beef now as he locks a cartridge
   in his rifle and aims it midway
   between the eyes while the cow
   watches and moos, and suddenly
   the shot—and the cow collapsing
   like a creature losing its footing
   on ice, its legs skedaddling
   right and left and under,
   and the farmer bracing to slit
   the gullet with a butcher knife
   and then the belly at the girth,
   his one arm bloody to the elbow
   as he digs for what is due
   to suckle in a day or two,
   and there it comes—a bullcalf
   black and white and unexpectedly
   alive, its meek hooves paired,
   its eyes half-open and its body
   fully formed but feeble in its own
   perfection as it lies almost
   angelic on the crimson straw.

As a Rule

Victors annoy me.
                        They overdo
    their victories with too much puffery.
I'm more inclined to share
    the universal lot of losers,
    not out of sympathy but frankly
    in the name of candor.
                        Losers
    have the look of men and women
    in their natural predicament—
    patient, sullen, luckless
    and determined.
                        Call it the look
    of ultimate acceptance.
                        It shows
    how unmistakably we sculpt
    our truest profile in defeat.
And history agrees.
                        Not every
    country haloed its heroes
    with laurel.
                        China for centuries
    found soldiers deserving
    of pity, even in triumph.
Aztecs honored their champions
    by sacredly beheading them.
Was this their way to prove
    no head could swell if there were
    no head there?
                        Or that
    the temporary anguish of defeat
    was less deplorable than braggadocio?

Or that the once defeated
    could arise triumphant from their chains,
    as history confirms they do,
    to prove that victories are brief?
Some take exception to such views,
    but, as a rule, they're true.

For the Dead, It's Over

They're spared the fretting and the raging
   that prevent us from surrendering
   at last to sleep, or paging
   through the past, or silencing
   an argument we're always waging
   with ourselves like Hamlet
   in a play we keep re-staging
   differently each time it plays
   to let us dream we're disengaging
   from whatever fate or fear
   awaits us in our aging.

Because the fear of aging
   makes us deal with death
   without a way of disengaging
   or pretending it's a dream,
   we always end by paging
   God to help us help
   ourselves and keep us waging
   our rebellion like an actor near
   the middle of the final staging
   of a play that ends before
   its time and leaves us raging.

Morituri

1

A man we loved is gone,
  a car he drove belongs
  to someone else, his house
  is up for sale, and we confront
  mortality each time we breathe.
Reduced to tears by memory,
  we learn the lost are always
  with us.
          And so they are
since love's the legacy of loss
and loss alone.
          What's past
lives on to prove the legacy
will last.
        But where's the clemency
in that?
        Without the right
to bid or pass, we're picked
to play the merciless poker
of chance, and the cards, the cards
keep coming, joker by joker.

2

It's forty days to the day,
  and you're not here.
            Last night
I called your number by mistake

and heard your still recorded
   message . . ."You have reached . . ."
It all came back—intensive
   care for days, one doctor
   who confirmed the truth, the nurses
   tending you as if you were
   their brother more than mine.
And all you asked was, "Sam,
   help me, for Christ's sake . . .
   I never wanted it to end
   like this."
                And nothing else.
The day was the Epiphany, surnamed
   Little Christmas.
                Monitors
   beside your bed recorded blood
   pressure, pulse, and every breath.
Before we left for lunch,
   we said our hesitant goodbyes.
You slept sedated, but the nurse
   assured us you could hear.
The last to speak was Sam,
   who carried both our names
   as dearest his mother insisted
   and whom you loved the most.
"Uncle Robert, we all love you,
   but now we're leaving for a bite
   to eat, and if you have
   to go while we're not here,
   it's okay . . . we'll understand."
He kissed your forehead twice,
   then held you in his arms.
Ten seconds later you were gone,
   as if his words had given you
   permission.

Later he told me
you parted your eyelids,
and your eyes were blue, not brown
as we had known them all your life.
No one could account for that.

3

Some say the three worst things
are losing a child, a mate
or a brother or sister.
                        Some say
the order's right, some say
it's wrong, but what's the point?
All losses to the losers stab alike
because they're all the worst.

4

You're buried in the same plot
with our uncle, our cousin, both
grandparents, our young mother,
and our great aunt who raised us
when our mother died and made us
what we were and are.
                        In the end
it came to family after all.
By intuition or epiphany,
you picked your gravesite decades
in advance as if you somehow
knew what none of us
could know.
                Just weeks before
you died, you said that death
no longer scared you though

you feared it all your life.
Later, we honored your bequests
   and sorted through your papers
   and effects.
                  We learned you were
the same in public as you were
at home—but more so.
                  What else
is there to say except,
   "So long for now, dear Bob."
Since brothers are forever brothers,
   you're here and elsewhere all the time
   for me exactly as you are
   and always were—but more so.

            For Robert George Hazo

Gloria

This seeing the sick endears them to us, us too it endears.
—Gerard Manley Hopkins

Named after Swanson the star,
  she knew good actresses from bad
  and did some acting herself.
But that was years before
  the three-pronged cane, the walker
  and the wheeled and cushioned chair.
"Sometimes I could scream," she said,
  "but why, what good would it do?"
Everything declinable declined
  except her will.
                    The nurses
were amazed, "We've never cared
for anyone like her."
                    Roses
  brought her to tears as did
  the memories of those she loved.
She aimed a special scorn
  at frauds and hypocrites.
                    "Some women
  marry money, and there's a name
  for that . . ."
                    "If being Christian
  means forgiving someone
  who harmed anyone I loved
  and never even apologized,
  I think that's asking a lot . . ."
At eighty-two she hated
  "being trouble for the nurses,"
  who already loved her frankness
  and her bold contempt of death.

To anyone who came to visit,
   she would smile and say, "Still here."
If dying were a play—and that
   her final line—, she said it
   jauntier than Swanson ever could.
Those selfsame words said something
   surer and beyond denial
   when she died.
                    The nurses understood.

   For Gloria Abdou

Skin-Deep Is Deep Enough

*The sight of a naked woman makes me think
of her skeleton.*
                    —Gustave Flaubert

Flaubert can speak for himself.
To me the sight of a naked
   woman overwhelms what passes
   for composure.
                    Women, of course,
   would see no more than just
   another of their gender—everything
   the same in general but different
   in specifics.
                    Most men would focus
   solely on specifics.
                    But where's
   the fault in that?
                    I've had
   my fill of puritans who claim
   we're only human from the waist
   up.
          They're always left
   to cope with interruptions from the waist
   down.
          I say we're not
   so halved, that honest passion
   is as civilized as reason
   and that all who mumble their denials
   face frustrations that denial breeds.
I find them cold in moments
   of affection, drawn to violence
   and totally devoid of mirth.
They have the villainies of soldiers

isolated and removed from all
refinements that define our happiness.
The regimen's no different for assassins,
  heavyweights preparing for a bout,
  and all who scourge their bodies
  in the name of God.
                         Frankly,
  the sins of Casanova pale
  beside the cruelties of chaste
  fanatics hardened by suppression.
Meanwhile the body's blamed
  for what suppression caused . . .
And yet, indulgers in excess
  seem no less hardened at the end.
St. Augustine of Hippo, Xavier,
  and John Donne condemned
  in retrospect the dreams of love
  that women roused in men.
Preparing to be dead, they preached
  renunciation of the flesh in sermons
  brilliant but depressing.
                         Why?
Who finds deliverance in shame?
I own two sculptures that suggest
  the opposite.
                    One is the head
of a woman carved from black
marble.
              Her nose is Romanly
bridgeless, her eyes lidded
and her neck like a dancer's arched
as far back as possible.
If she is dreaming, she will dream
  forever.
                The second is a torso

in limestone—headless, armless,
legless.
      From neck to breasts
to hips, what's true of women
everywhere seems even truer
in the shameless nudity of stone.
I have no interest in her skeleton.

The World That Waits in Words

Looking back or forward
  never works.
              Distortion
poisons hindsight, and presumption
renders foresight unreliable.
Right now is all that's real,
  and that's just time enough
  to live without revision or analysis.
Deafened and dulled by the dead
  words of the living, I read
  the living words of the dead
  (plus two beyond cajolery)
  for guidance.
           And guidance it is.
Their books are there to be
  consulted when the need
  demands it.
          I learn from them
what lovers learn from love
but find impossible to say.
It's like a silence to be shared
  as secrets, gifts, or meals
  are shared.
         Otherwise, nothing
is different.
       The news is bad,
the market volatile, the weather
sunny and the traffic heavy.
Cowards are shrewder than heroes,
  and long outlive them.
          Talkers
outnumber doers.

One
out of ten of us is marked
for sudden death while all
the other nine will linger.
War
and executions qualify as lawful
murders, but who shall say so?
Yesterday in consultation with Camus,
I mentioned how absurd it is
to know such facts and not
despair.
Camus replied
that consciousness is all—just
consciousness—despite the odds.
This morning I reviewed Pascal
and found his wager with God
a sensible conclusion.
Later
I'll visit Richard Wilbur.
And tomorrow?
Tomorrow I'll re-read a poem
by Szymborska and learn how poetry
can polka even in the midst
of sadness, madness, and confusion.

For Jo McDougall

And the Time Is

We have come to the point of decision,
   and the hands of the clock say—be careful.
We've learned from the past that our choices
   are one or the other or neither,
   and the hands of the clock say—be careful.
We have readied ourselves for the challenge
   by weighing the odds and the chances
   of what will result from our choices,
   and the hands of the clock say—be hopeful.

We're not what we were when we started,
   and the hands of the clock say—it's over.
Our yesterdays lengthen like shadows
   that fade when we no longer cast them,
   and the hands of the clock say—it's over.
Despite what it brings to surprise us,
   we treasure each day in its passing
   though we know that we pass as it passes,
   and the hands of the clock say—discover.

We sit on the porch every evening,
   and the hands of the clock say—be watchful.
We study the leaves in their turning
   from green to vermilion to purple,
   and the hands of the clock say—be watchful.
While we stare at the sky in its vastness
   and name every star in the distance,
   we dwindle to scale in the balance,
   and the hands of the clock say—be grateful.

The dead come to life in our living,
   and the hands of the clock say—remember.

The words of a prophet keep haunting
    the ones who ignored him when living,
    and the hands of the clock say—remember.
The world that we think is around us
    is neither before nor behind us
    but always within us, within us,
    and the hands of the clock say—forever.

Once, Again

Each April is the same
 but somehow greener every year.
Lovers who've made love
 on hundreds of nights anticipate
 the next loving as their first.
Shaving for the twenty-seven
 thousandth time on the Fourth
 of another July should be
 no different, but it is.
                        Breakfast
 today, although identical
 with yesterday's, is one day
 better.
            Even these words
 have predecessors by the millions
 from my very hand, but still
 I write them as the first
 and final words I'll write.
Some say I should be bored.
If so, I should be bored
 with breathing, but I'm not.
If you believe hereafter's
 here already, and that now
 is always now, you'd say
 the same.
            And you'd be right.

Sudden or Slow but Sure

Wounded by shrapnel in France
  six decades back, he's still
  recovering from trauma caused
  by trauma.
                  In every book
by Edward Wood he resurrects
the pain.
            When Hemingway received
the wound that made him think
at Fassalta de Piave, the outcome
was the same: re-living
and re-telling what was sudden,
merciless and permanent.
                      It's not
confined to war.
            Preparing
for a trip to Europe, Reynolds
Price complained of cramping
in his lower back.
            X-rays
confirmed a shadow.
              Days
later he awoke from surgery
a paraplegic.
          Shock was the first
response, then transformation.
                  Bernard
Costello cased his saxophone
to specialize in oral surgery
after his dearest friend
was mangled in a crash.
             H. R.
survived a stroke but lived

a posthumous existence to the end.
And there was Frank the catcher.
Built like a heavyweight, he stood
  akimbo when he spoke, flexing
  his jaw as if each word
  were like a throw to second.
First-string at twenty on the college
  varsity, he'd been approached
  by scouts and was inclined.
Struck later in the jaw
  by a ball thrown wild and hard,
  he changed.
              Thirty pounds
  lighter with a wired jawbone
  and six teeth lost, he seemed
  uncertain to the point of deference.
The list has no amen.
              To trump
  the odds, discretion matters less
  than valor, which matters less
  than zero where absurdity's concerned.
The ultimate defense is luck.
The ultimate reprieve is luck.

The Contrarians

On the one hand, cure—
   the hopes and risks of cure.
Otherwise, predictable pain—
   ongoing, sudden or ultimate.
Only a masochist would opt
   for pain—and a strong masochist
   at that.
           But what if cure
   becomes a lesser or even
   worse choice than pain?
Griffin, the diabetic, learned
   that amputation of one leg
   would add a decade to his life.
"Forget the years," he said,
   "I'd rather die—entire . . ."
Knowing she had to drive him
   ninety miles for dialysis
   thrice weekly, Sigmund decided
   it was time.
           The drive was aging
   Jane, and all for what?
One night he said, "Enough's
   enough," and then he kissed her.
For eight more days they were
   as close as ever. . . .
           Trapped
   high in the South Tower
   with no way down or up
   and fire and smoke behind,
   they held each other's hands
   like newlyweds a hundred
   floors above Manhattan
   in September and jumped. . . .

To those who say survival
   is the highest law of life,
   I offer the above.
                    Plus one . . .
Soldiers have risked or sacrificed
   their lives to save the lives
   of men they could have just
   let die.
          Call theirs an act
   of greater love or call it
   anything you please.
                    To all
   who claim that life amounts
   to nothing more than not dying,
   I say there are exceptions.

PART FIVE
The Short Life of Perpetuity

The Fifth Element

Three we find as given.
One we make.
                    And the fifth?
The fifth presents a problem.
The earth is waiting to be tamed,
  seeded, tunneled, or plowed.
Water is ours for drinking,
  bathing, cooking, or sailing.
The air makes vassals of us all,
  and fire will kindle on demand
  from nothing into flame and ash.
But clouds?
                 As spume or spray
or white ascensions billowing
through space or thunderheads
as sudden as volcanic smoke,
they hug the world like works
in progress.
                 What's happening beneath
repeats the travesty called history:
genocide in Africa, regiments
drugged by uniforms and slogans,
governments ruled by democratically
elected undermen or thugs.
The clouds slur over them
  indifferently.
                 Surnamed in Latin
as cumulus, nimbus, cirrus
and stratus, they even sound
like facts in motion.
                 And that's
their secret.

Mountains arise
in place and stay there.
                    Rivers
surrender to the sea and never
leave.
          Fires that flare
and blaze into infernos rarely
last for long.
               And what
is air but mere transparency?
But clouds create themselves
in pilgrimage and never twice
the same.
          They shadow all
they cover and are gone.
                    Like all
the best of guests, they're briefly
in attendance.
               They keep their proper
distance, hover and move on.

In Troth

Forget the birthdays.
                    For me
    you're younger than ever.
                        Nothing
    is truer than that.
                    Tonight
    I thought of life without you,
    and I died—no one to kid
    or kiss, no one to say
    that blue is not my color,
    no one to shuck mussels with
    from the same bowl, no one
    to live the patience that is love
    in waiting.
                    You're always new
    to know—a mate I choose
    all over every day.
                        You make
    our lives seem one long day
    with no past tense.
                        I love you
    for the times you've slowed me down
    before I would have blundered.
I love you for the hundred ways
    you saw what I would
    never see until you'd seen it
    first.
            We're nip and tuck,
    saddle and boot, a pair
    of gloves, a study in rhyme
    from A to Z without a flub
    between.

We're grateful so
for one lone son whose music
loops the globe, grandchildren
three, and Dawn who keeps
all five in love together
and intact.
    If I could make
right now eternal as a song,
I would.
    Impossible, of course.
But not the wanting to . . .
       That's why
I want impossibility to last,
regardless.
   That's happiness.

Making It Look Easy

Whatever it is, Spencer Tracy
  had it—acting as if he wasn't
  acting, which is acting at its best.
So did Fred Astaire and Ginger Rogers
  swirling in "The Continental," Bojangles
  tapping, Michael Jackson
  at his peak, Nureyev leaping
  and Gene Kelly on his own.
Sampras in his prime made sport
  and grace synonymous.
                     Seferis
in Beirut preserved within himself
the Greece the Nazis never
could defeat.
              Greece lives forever
and wherever in his poetry.
                   And that's
the point.
          There's one Seferis
to a century, if that.
                The same
is true of those named
heretofore who made a poem
of their work.
            Why bother with less
when nothing better than the best
should ever be imagined?
               Let those
who say that poetry is mere
technique be damned.
             They're thinking
only of the tricks that inspiration
nixes with impunity to let

perfection happen. . . .
                          I had
an uncle who was tops in pool.
No one could match him.
                          Thirty
years retired from the game,
he took a pool shark's challenge
as a dare.
                  Without a session
to rehearse, he chalked his cue,
then broke the rack and ran
the table as of old.
                          The bet
was made and paid, and that
was that.
                  Even the loser
was amazed to watch a master
show him how poetically
the art of 8-ball could be played.

The Short Life of Perpetuity

Amin Maalouf could write:
   "Our sole consolation, before
   being laid to rest, is to have loved
   and been loved, and perhaps
   to have left a personal trace."
Commendable, of course.
                      Not quite
   as slick as a lyric by Cole
   Porter but basically true.
Translated, it means how all
   that's once and only supersedes
   what pleases in passing but never
   fulfills.
          And I agree.
Show me whoever balks
   at being loved or loving back,
   I'll show you a fool.
                But what's
   "a personal trace?"
              For men
   it might be hoping to be profiled
   on a coin or stamp or having airports,
   parks or boulevards perpetuate
   their names.
          Most women
   could care less.
           For them to know
   that those most dear to them
   are well and happy is memorial
   enough.
        They see the rest
   as vanity or rational stupidity.

If moments lived are not
   their own reward, then what's
   the point?
                    Clark Gable
   knew the difference.
                         Idolized
   by millions in his prime, he spoke
   dismissively of stardom—"I eat
   and use the bathroom like everybody."
When asked what kind of funeral
   he'd want, he snorted, "Don't make
   a circus out of it."
                    Recently
   I asked a group of undergraduates
   if they remembered Clark Gable.
None did except one girl who said,
   "I think I've heard the name."
Gable would have smiled at that.

Kennedy

I came before they built
　　the monument, and what I saw
　　was scarcely monumental: sloped
　　grass on either shoulder
　　of the road that curved and banked
　　below an overpass, the book building
　　overlooking ordinary traffic
　　patterns on an ordinary Friday
　　of an ordinary March, the skyline
　　clouding ordinarily to rain . . .
One shot missed, but two
　　hit, according to reports.
Cheap rifle, moving target,
　　lone shooter firing down,
　　re-aiming twice—the facts
　　defied ballistics and belief.
Later I saw post mortem
　　photos of his face unmarked
　　by exit wounds or evidence
　　of impact.
　　　　　　Questions, controversy,
　　suppositions. . . .
　　　　　　　Following his route,
I passed a billboard opposite
the first trajectory.
　　　　　　　An ordinary
billboard.
　　　　　That must have been
the final thing he saw.

The Fools of God

If certain politicians come
　　across as serious jokes,
　　what's left for you to do
　　but say so while you frown
　　and laugh?
　　　　　　　Not that it changes
anything, but then who knows?
At worst it lets you add
　　some further cautions to your creeds.
On poetry, carpentry, dance
　　and sports—the art is not
　　to show the art.
　　　　　　　On help—
too much too soon, too little
too late.
　　　　　On destiny—life
matters more than death
since life's explorable while death's
unknowable and final.
　　　　　　　　On weapons—
gun owners should be forced
by law to learn to play
the violin.
　　　　　　On money—what's earned
is truer than what's gifted or won
by luck.
　　　　　On fate—all
that we learn in retrospect
is worthless in the present tense.
Call these the credos of a fool
　　in any commonwealth whose only
　　gods are acquisition or celebrity,
　　and you'd be right.

Regardless,
when courage or conformity are all
the options left, most fools
courageously disdain conformity
and dare to face the odds.
That's why they're fools to everyone
except themselves.
They know
they're closest to the truth
when what they say arouses
mockery while not a soul applauds.

The Merchandiser's Song

Sell only the best for as much as you can
and make it appear like a bargain from God.
It takes as much work to sell rubies as toothpicks,
but watch how the difference quintuples your profits
and let that convince you the difference is worth it.
I've done this for years so I know what I'm saying.

It's true that men buy, but smart women shop,
which means that they notice while men merely look.
When choosing a car, a woman will favor
a color that makes it the key to the deal,
and the man has no choice but to buy it to please her.
I've dealt with all kinds so I know what I'm saying.

With Arabs you haggle, with Brits you're exact.
Don't deal with Chinese, or you're certain to lose.
A Frenchman in business is cold but correct.
A Spaniard stays calm unless he feels cheated,
but if he feels cheated, you better leave town.
I've traveled a lot so I know what I'm saying.

Don't brag of your gains, or you'll gain the wrong friends.
When you lose, you'd be wise not to mention your losses.
Gripe, and you'll find that you bore your defenders
and gladden all those who were happy you flopped.
Look up when you're down, look down when you're up.
I've lost and I've won so I know what I'm saying.

If men need to choose for today or tomorrow,
they'll choose for today, and tomorrow can wait.
This means that you sell them what tempts them right now
before they can muster a reason to tell you

they would if they could or thanks, but no thanks.
I've learned how men think so I know what I'm saying.

Selling yourself is a game without mercy.
If nobody buys, you're equal to zero.
The name of the game is how much you are worth.
If you make a million, you're worth what you've made.
If you take in nothing, you're not worth a thing.
I've sold my whole life so I know what I'm saying.

Sloth Is the Mother of Invention

Because he tired of climbing stairs,
   Otis invented elevators
   which invented skyscrapers
   which converted downtown Chicago,
   Dallas, and New York into downtown
   Chicago, Dallas, and New York . . .
Intrigued with automobility,
   Henry Ford produced the horseless
   carriage that promoted sanitation
   plus convenience.
                 No more manure
   on city streets.
                 More speed,
  less shoveling.
                 Stench became
a memory, and people drove
while sitting statue-still behind
a wheel. . . .
                 Plumbing and flushable
commodes made dumping chamber
pots defunct while buttoned
or zippered trouser-flies for men
and skirts for women sensibly
facilitated urination. . . .
                 Dismissive
of negotiations and slow wars,
   Hitler simply blitzed his enemies.
If might made right, why bother
  with diplomacy?
                 Diplomacy took time,
  and time took effort, and effort
  meant time wasted if war
  could cut the time in half. . . .

Show me a shortcut, and I'll prove
   how only people steeped
   in laziness could give us elevators,
   autos—toilets—clothing
   tailored for hygiene—and war
   and be proclaimed, for good
   or ill or both, ingenious.

Blossom

I sing of Blossom in her proud
  and permanent prime.
                    She celebrates
  one hundred and three birthdays
  by wearing crimson lipstick
  and designer eyewear a la Gucci.
She's had her white hair bobbed
  beneath a crowning scarf.
She's totally lost count of every
  President she voted for, outlived
  and left to history.
                    In photographs
  she smiles with all her original
  teeth.
          Dismissive of dotage,
  she chooses wardrobes that are right
  for her and her alone,
  as in her preference for lingerie
  a generation east of Mae West.
She leaves no room for doubt.
After her oldest daughter
  mentioned that she'd changed her will,
  Blossom asked her with a smile,
  "What did you leave me?"

Welcome to Used-to-Was

After you pass the Orthodontic
   Center near the Chrysler dealership,
   you'll see an Apostolic Church
   between two blocks of Civil War
   frame-houses with flags
   a-flutter from every porch,
   a neon sign that welcomes
   hunters, and all that's left
   of an old Sunoco station
   gone to weeds and desolation
   near a second Apostolic Church
   that used to be a clinic
   for sick dogs.
              The locals call
this village Used-to-Was because
the way it is is not
the way it was.
             Storefronts
are boarded up for sale or rent
except for one that offers
cigarettes, cold beer, and porn,
an office selling bail-bonds
by appointment, and markets hawking
shooting duds for hunters in deer
season.
           The highway leading
into town becomes Main Street,
which has the same three stoplights
that it's had since the Depression.
If all the lights are green
   your next time by, it takes
   two minutes—plus or minus—
   and you're in and through and out.

Tattoos

They once were seen as trademarks
  of distinction for sailors.
                            Lately
  they're everywhere you look.
For men—lightning zigzags
  on the ankles, deltas of Venus
  where chin meets chest, American
  flags on shoulder blades or cocks.
For women—a blue and smiling
  moon sequestered in the small
  of the back, roses on the upper
  ass, a Christian cross
  between the breasts, or an arrow
  pointing southward from the navel.
Cannibals believed tattoos
  distinguished them from beasts.
But now who knows if each
  tattoo's a badge or just
  graffiti with an attitude?
                           Some
  call it body art.
                 Some say
  it's ink on meat.
               If no
  erasing laser's in the cards,
  it's there for keeps, which means
  it's guaranteed to last for life
  and in the grave.
               It never sleeps.

The King of Swing

They tromp on stage in fours
   with amplified guitars low slung
   and aimed at fans who clap
   and yelp and ought to know
   better.
           Add flashing lights
   and smoke, and there's the formula.
What's total din for me
   is ecstasy for them, and tens
   of thousands pay to hear it. . . .
Give me the years of Benny
   Goodman in his prime.
                 I
   saw him twice but loved
   his music long before
   I saw him once: Krupa
   on drums, Hampton on vibes
   and Teddy Wilson on piano.
To show he could, he guested
   with the Philharmonic and performed
   the Paganini variations to a tee.
The night I saw him last
   he let the spotlight stay
   on Ziggy Elman's trumpet
   dialogues with Krupa's paradiddles.
He listened like a king in shadow,
   snapping his fingers and tapping
   his toes.
           Watching him prime
   his clarinet and prep his reed,
   we waited like the amateurs we were
   to hear the solo that we knew
   would come.

And when it came,
we heard a maestro in performance
at his best, unamplified and perfect.

Say Cheese

You force a smile until
    you think you look the way
    you think you look.
                    The man
    behind the camera wants
    a bigger smile, and you comply
    as to a dentist's, "Open wider."
For smiles to qualify as smiles,
    the eyes and lips must rhyme,
    but now your eyes resign
    from the equation.
                    Plain vanity
    sustains the shot, and authenticity
    be damned.
                    You hold the pose.
Since posing is what posing
    does, you learn that all
    that posing does is mold you
    in a pose the poser wants.
For just that long, you're who
    you're not.
                    When you unpose
    and are yourself again,
    you see what made the Iroquois
    believe that being photographed
    permitted the photographer to steal
    your soul.
                    The Iroquois were right.

Sleep Is a Dangerous Exile

Watches, shoes and outer garb?
Superfluous.
                Loose-fitting cottons
   will do or nothing at all,
   depending on the thermostat.
Some claim that sleep's the ultimate
   democracy this side of death
   although it wastes one-third
   of every day and every life
   in deference to nothing but fatigue.
Asleep, you feel defenseless
   and alone.
             Nightmares
   will stun you like a storm at sea,
   quicksand will suck you
   under, and the dead will rise.
It's more than Freudian suppression
   that's at work.
             It's life's ongoing
   war against itself, and you're
   the victim.
            The lone escape
   is waking up.
            You leave
   your dreams the way a swimmer
   leaves the ocean, no longer
   threatened by that element.
               But dangers
   never die, and you will swim
   those depths again. . . .
            Remember
   the swerving car that almost
   ran you down?

It grazed you
like a passing curse and smeared
its fender salt like whitewash
on your coat.
                An inch here,
an inch there. . . .
                    But in your dreams
you're always hit.
                Your coat's
entangled with a tire.
                    You're being
dragged and mangled by the wheels.
The driver speeds away
  but not from guilt or fear
of being found at fault.
                    It seems
he never even saw you.

Heredity's a Card That's Always Dealt Face Down

I met the daughter of a daughter
  of a student from an English class
  I offered fifty years ago.
Like someone overtaken in a race,
  I felt both far behind and dated.
Appearing older with the young
  but younger with the old is how
  I see myself these days.
But what's the point?
                    Are years
  from birth more relevant than history?
I trace my mother's heritage
  to great grandparents only,
  and my father's to his father—
  no farther back than that.
My nameless predecessors vanish
  in Darwinian oblivion.
                    Or do they?
Whatever they were, I am.
Who knows what heathens, heroes,
  Homers, hookers, Hitlers
  hunters, holier-than-thouers,
  hacks or hicks or humpbacks
  hide like secrets in my genes?
I'm just the next progenitor
  whose future is a past to come.
If that's the formula, why fret?
Between the randomly begotten
  and the soon to be forgotten,
  I expect I'll be remembered only
  as the temporary presence known
  as me and, even then, dismissively.

Eyes

Startled like a girl surprised
  in her shower, the doe defied
  my stare.
           Animal to animal,
  we cancelled distance with our eyes.
For just that long I learned
  how much the present differs
  from presence.
             The present is
  what's here right now while
  presence is what's always here.
Lifting her foreleg to flee,
  the doe remained hoof-deep
  in shallows while we listened
  to each other with our eyes.
               Fleet
  as an echo that lessens to nil,
  the listening lingered and lingered. . . .
It's lingering still.
          That's presence.

A Preferable Nudity

Goya's Majas, for example. . . .
The one in clothes would likely
  be ashamed unclothed.
                      The one
  that's nude would be defiled
  clothed.
          This proves the naked
and the nude are not the same.
A poem fraught with artifice
  before it's shorn of everything
  superfluous invites denuding
  from the start.
               What's left at last
  might not be poetry at all.
A poem in the nude affirms
  its nudity without disguise.
It's absolute in all its spareness
  down to what defies
  addition or subtraction or indifference.
The Maja in her finery and shoes
  presents a woman hidden
  by the muting camouflage of fashion.
The Maja nude reveals
  a woman's total face
  in perpetuity unhidden and aloud
  from eyebrows down to toes.
Adornment would insult it.

The Art Professor Discusses Bernini's *Teresa in Ecstasy*

Depicting her, Bernini did not sculpt
   the woman who would counsel popes
   or dance flamenco in the convent
   when the nuns were bored.
                          Instead,
   he focused solely on her face
   contorted in an agony of pleasure,
   her eyes half-lidded
   and her parted lips unwilling
   to return the oval of her mouth
   to silence.
             A bride outspread
   and straddling her lover's loins
   would look like this, her body
   primed for what she hopes will happen
   and desires more than breath
   itself.
          It's possible Bernini
   watched or fantasized a woman
   locked in such a wild tussle.
Why not transfer this image
   to a sainted nun?
              With consummation
   as his parable, Bernini carved Teresa
   swooning in God's orgy
   as any woman might when yielding
   to a love both wanton and permissible.

The Time It Takes to Tell

Posing *contrapposto* for the class,
    she seemed to say, "I'm here
    in body, but the rest of me
    is otherwhere."
                    And why not?
Standing nude for minimum wage
    invites escape.
                    Her breasts
    and hips were fortyish, her pubes
    a darker auburn than her bangs,
    her appendectomy not quite obscure.
Regardless, the music of a woman's
    body sang in her, contained
    and hinted at like rubies in a purse.
Some of the student painters
    caught it on their canvases—echoes
    of de Milo or the shameless Maja.
The model herself seemed unaware
    of what her body meant.
During a break she asked
    what time it was: "I never
    wear a watch at work because
    a watch would make me look
    not naked."
                    I thought no more
    of that as she resumed her role
    as Woman in the name of all
    her gender.
                    Posed, her body
    changed into a bet that said,
    "While the loser in me says
    I just might win, the winner
    tells me I could lose."

That seemed to leave her motionless
   in mid-bet, shielded like a secret
   in the sisterhood of female skin
   while being re-created on a dozen
   easels.
            The silence in the studio
   was almost churchly.
                        Later,
   with the class dismissed and she
   alone and bare, she found
   her watch and strapped it on her wrist.
And just as suddenly as that,
   she seemed no longer naked.

Flagrante Delicto

Downriver from the Pont
  du Gard while tourists parked
  to picnic on the banks and benches,
  and a multilingual guide explained
  how arches of the aqueduct were built
  with stones as old as Rome,
  a woman and a man embraced
  and grappled in the shelter of a cove
  where they had hung their clothes
  like laundry on an olive branch
  until they coupled at the loins
  and kept each other in a clasp
  much older than a hundred Romes
  in open view from the opposite
  shore of a villa chosen
  once by Richelieu for a visit
  called official by its current
  owners now in Avignon
  just as their gardener, observing
  totally by chance the doings
  on the shore below, removed
  his gloves to light his cigarette
  and, braced against his planted
  shovel, smoked and watched.

The Face of Catherine Deneuve

French without question—a smile
  that's nine parts mirth
  and one part doubt, the chin
  untucked and the left eyebrow
  arched a fraction.
                 Never
a different face in public
than in private, never a pose . . .
She sees whatever is there
  as if she's seen it twice
  too many times to be
  impressed.
             And that's what you
recall as you recall a French
woman's way of dismissing nonsense
with a click of her lips.
               In films
she's totally indifferent to how
beautiful she is.
                It's not an act.
And there's no need for nudity
  to bare the woman within.
The face is nude enough
  to speak in every alphabet
  plus silence.
            Silence especially . . .
When someone noted that Deneuve
  had perfect features, a connoisseur
  from Montparnasse demurred
  with a smile, "Not perfect, but better."

Ophelia's Lie

Not that her innocence and age
    were an excuse . . .
                After all,
    the girl could hold her own
    in argument, dispute her brother's
    platitudes and sing Elizabethan
    songs while strumming on a lute.
And she was beautiful as girls
    in adolescence are before they realize
    how beautiful they are.
                  What ended
    everything was when she let
    herself be used and then
    denied it to his face.
                He never
    was the same . . .
                It took so little
    to destroy so much the way
    a microscopic but malignant speck
    can wreck a body, or a misprint
    maim a poem or a name.

Sloth Is a Lost Art

You thought you'd take to menus
   a la carte with service, room
   and tax included in a pre-paid
   package—and the climate the same
   from day to day.
               You practiced
what believers call the virtue
of abandonment.
               And for a time
it helped.
           You totally forgot
what Brando's folly in Tahiti
prophesied.
            He bought an island
where he had the sea desalinated,
ordered what he ate flown in
and woke each day to propagate
the race.
          Short-lived as WALDEN
but less noble, the outcome
was the same.
           The sea sailed back
to salt, the dinners spoiled
in flight, and all the virgins
in Tahiti mated, mothered,
aged and in the process went
to fat. . . .
        For you the change
was not as radical.
            Lounging
every day became a day
too long.

You hungered for the phone
to ring.
Monday was Thursday
was Sunday.
Rest as a way
of life was hardly a match
for the Protestant ethic.
Moreover,
Eden without its snake became
a bore.
It made you think
that boredom must have made
one apple seem more succulent
to Eve than usual.
Or so
she dreamed.
According to the myth,
our history began when Eve
succumbed to something tempting
on a whim.
The choice was simpler
when it came to him.
Since he
had nothing much to think about
and no experience at all
with apples, consequence or women,
Adam bit.
And that was it.

No Words for This

If a true poem is one
   you wish you never had
   to write, then this is it.
Don't read it just to say
   you've read it.
                That's like
the traveler who went to Spain
so he could say he went
to Spain.
             The words I've picked
have really picked themselves,
but what's not written here
is where the poem breathes. . . .
The mother of a captain killed
   by snipers read his final
   letter postmarked on the date
   he died.
          She read it often
after that.
            And every time
she closed the envelope, she slowly
licked it shut so that her tongue
could taste him in the last
thing he ever touched.

Skunked

Alamo, Great Wall or Maginot—
   they all were breached, bypassed
   or broken.
                   Generals like Foch
condemned such barriers as futile
and extolled attack.
                      But somehow
   all attackers fail when conquests
   burgeon into burdens, and the victims
   mount rebellions and prevail.
Thucydides and Hemingway implied
   we're worse in war than beasts
   that only kill from need and never
   with malice.
                  Are we that base?
Is strength the vice we copy
   from the lion?
                   Guile from the fox?
Deception from the leopard?
                     Stealth
   from the wolf?
                Or is this listing
   too selective since it overlooks
   the sane and self-reliant skunk?
He keeps his enemies at bay
   and stays untouched in the peace
   of the totally repugnant.
                    Cornered,
   he's ready to scuttle the bother
   of battle and show the perceptive
   few that stench is the perfect
   weapon of choice for the bullied—
   bloodless, inexpensive, and effective.

Executioner

The guillotining blade was slanted
  to permit a perfect slice.
You probably have seen engravings
  where a bucket waits
  to catch the severed head.
One wonders who the sadist was
  behind this method of dispatch.
And by what God or government
  commended?
          In fact, a doctor—
Joseph Ignace Guillotin.
He thought beheadings merciful
  compared to crucifixions, being
  drawn and quartered, cracked
  on a rack, roped to a post
  and torched, or tugged to pieces
  by horses.
        He claimed a prisoner
  would feel a feathery touch
  at the nape of his neck, no more.
Gravity would do the rest.

Man Is the Only Animal Capable of Shame

Man is the beast with red cheeks.
—Friedrich Nietzsche

I watched on film a pride
  of lions feasting on a water
  buffalo they'd overwhelmed.
                          They ripped
  and clawed the carcass into shreds.
They cracked the bones.
                    Not one
  was penitent.
              Later they slept
  or roamed or copulated in the open.
No matter what they did, they did it
  in their naked skin and shamelessly.
Not us.
        Consequence, not subsequence,
  defines our lives, and consequences
  mean that no one has the option
  of impunity.
              Our vices drive us
  to addiction or repentance.
                          Killers,
  liars, thieves and traitors
  have been known to suffer genuine
  remorse when facing their accusers.
This proves there still can be
  contrition even from the worst.
Never to rollick like lions
  in public, we're racked by appetites
  and conscience, and the price for deviance
  is guilt.

Anguish returns us
to our suddenly awaiting
lives where we're still human
after all.
           What saves us
from the worst that we can be
but shame?
           What keeps us
always who we are but shame—
the merciless justice of shame?

Signs of Life in a Sundown City

We number less than half of what
  we were four decades back.
The young look elsewhere for their lives.
The old grow older and die.
Mansions of a long dead gentry
  calcify like skulls.
                        Museums
  lease from millionaires what artists
  painted while they starved.
                        On streets
  that once were prime, the smell
  of oligarchy gone bourgeois is palpable.
The current synonym for blackjack,
  poker, craps and slots
  is gaming.
                Uptown at midnight
  the currency is drugs and guns,
  and murderers grow younger
  by the day.
                Regardless, the trees
  parade in place at permanent
  attention.
                Simply by happening,
  each day proclaims itself unique
  and unrepeatable.
                        And two
  undaunted rivers fork and fuse
  into a third that flows into a fourth
  that steers in silence to the sea
  that's stayed the same since Genesis.

Prior to Oblivion

Even the totally forgettable
  forgets to be forgotten.
                    Calling
  this regrettable but so, we live
  with echoes.
            How often have we
  fretted to recall a name,
  phone number or a face
  and come up blank?
               Since no one
  likes what's unacceptable, we blame
  the failure on fatigue or senioritis,
  but the cause is simpler than that.
Remembering four digits in a row
  is easy.
          Eleven is harder
  but possible.
              Forty's hopeless . . .
That's how it is with memory.
It chokes on gluttony and rids
  itself of dross by dumping
  the excess.
            If names and numbers
  vanish in the voiding, what's the loss?
Because the mind is made
  to make itself up and choose,
  the lesser trivia must go.
Knowing that the Great Wall
  of China is one thousand
  miles longer than America
  is wide is certainly of interest.
Noteworthy too that St. Augustine
  lived faithfully for nine years

with the mother of his bastard son.
But these are facts, just facts.
If we remember everything
   that's past, we'll fatten with data
   or be sluiced away like flotsam
   in a flood.
               Summering hummingbirds
   know better.
              They flash through space
   in perfect symmetry.
                 They savor
only the important flowers.
The rest are noticed but ignored.
Why name the many or the few
   they favor?
            Better to stress
how steadily they hover like tops
kept spinning in place at full
speed until they're ready
to power down, ponder and choose.

Malaise

It happens when you feel as old
   as those too old to care
   how old they are.
                 Bored
with everything but breakfast,
then sickened by the taste of toast,
you take your coffee black—
no sugar.
           This morning's headlines
echo yestermorning's headlines
to the letter.
          You read no further
to remind yourself that news
is never new.
         Each day is not
a time to live but time
to live through, and then
not always as you like.
           The Germans
have a word for this, as do
the French, who have a word
for everything.
         But then what
difference does it make to give
a name to what you feel
in two or twenty languages?
It's simply there.
         It lingers
like a stench that worsens by the day
until one night, without
a word or push from you,
it leaves as if it never
happened.

You wonder if it's gone
for good or if it ever was.
Later you come to understand how
you were wounded to the point
of madness from within, although
you stayed the man you are.
Compared to visible pain
and anguish, this is not unusual.
Torturers proficient in the skills
of malice have been known to leave
their victims broken and babbling
but unbloodied and without a scar.

Ars Poetica

I've had enough of poets
who repeatedly proclaim they're poets
and compose sestinas just to show
they can but never see that wordplay's
not the same as poetry, which matters
so much more since it confirms
that those who wield the pen
cannot help writing what they write
because the secrets that they learn
whenever they're inspired reveal
how poetry comes when it comes,
and when it comes, it comes
as unexpectedly as summer lightning,
and the few struck numb are dared
to say just once what only
rarely can be said at all,
but, dared or not, they strive
the way undaunted sculptors
carve and whittle masterpieces
out of ice although they're cautioned
in advance that warmer weathering
will swallow everything they sculpt
like substance silenced into shadow—
but still, but still they do it.

Poseidon and Others

His spear is somewhere sunk
  in the Aegean.
                The upraised hand
grips nothing.
                His body's primed
for hurling—Olympian legs
astride, both shoulders squared,
the bearded face straightforward,
and the eyes aiming.
                Why quibble
if antiquities are flawed—a nose
chipped, a penis broken
at its base, a finger gone,
the arms of Aphrodite amputated
just beneath the shoulders?
                Flawless,
they would show us totally
what David offers us in Florence
to a fault.
            Even when complete
the statues of the Greeks revealed
the breasts of all the Caryatids
unnippled and the eyes opaque.
The wearing down of centuries
  would do the rest.
             Whipping
without his whip in hand,
the charioteer of Delphi rides
the wind.
           The missing horse,
the whip, the chariot itself
have long since gone to ruin,

but the race that's never won
or lost has always just begun.

Home Are the Sailors

Like those who sail away and then
  come back, we keep returning
  to a port we've never left.
A life we used to live
  await us there as shores await
  all sailors home from sea.
So much is differently the same.
And yet what is the present
  but a future that the past
  made possible?
           There is
no older story.
           And what
are we but random pilgrims
  stopped in progress to remember?
It now seems more like then,
  why care?
         As long as home
means where we most belong—
  for just that long—we're there.

PART SIX
Deuce

Imperfectly Yours

Like ricochets the goldfish
　glide, hover and dive.
Nibbling surface-bubbles
　or bottom-feeding, they never
　collide.
　　　　In swirling flights
of geese I've seen the same
respect for space.
　　　　　　They form
a soaring vee—each one
positioned at a slant to slip
the wind-wakes from the geese
ahead.
　　　　Instinct explains it,
and yet there's more of mystery
than instinct here.
　　　　　　Compare it
to platoons of Fleet marines
in silent drill.
　　　　They march
in total unison without
a sound—their rifles spun,
smacked or shouldered in salutes,
their faces almost furious
with concentration.
　　　　　　While geese
do what they do without
instruction or command, the marchers
must rehearse and re-rehearse
to make the difficult look easy.
For geese, perfection's not an outcome
　but a gift.

To men so blest
and gifted as to make their actions
perfect every time they act,
we give the name of genius.
Whatever's perfect for the rest
of us means doing and re-doing.
We know before we start
that failure's just as likely
as success, which means that words
like these might not survive
Horace's nine reasons for revision.
That's why we marvel at the miracle
of Swedish swallows flying
over half of Europe and all
of Africa to the Cape of Good
Hope and back each year
without a mishap or a map.

Stoning

It fits.
        It lets my fingers
act like fingers as I flex
my aging bones around
a stone that's been the same
for years, for centuries, forever.
Sledged or morselized, it multiplies
    like grief.
           Cradled in a sling
and flung, it brings Goliaths
to their knees.
             Even in Genesis
its purpose was foretold when Cain
"rose up" against his twin
and cracked his skull.
               And this
continues.
        In Persia by another
name a woman "taken
in adultery" faces execution
for her sin.
         A ring of men
surrounds her like a closing
noose.
     Hooded and buried
upright to her breasts, she waits
for "one without fault"—her very
brother—"to cast the first stone."
Once thrown, think blood, think bone.

Life Preservers

He kept a fleet of Rolls Royce
  classic cars garaged like special
  stallions in a single stable.
Because Elizabeth the queen
  had ridden in one, he had
  the ride remembered on a plaque
  of silver mounted on the dash.
That's not as random as it sounds.
For memory's sake we treasure
  photographs, inscriptions, letters
  ribboned in a box and etchings
  on defiant tombstones.
                    It's called
commemoration.
                    Or do we mean
perpetuation—if not in perpetuity,
  then part way there at least?
But what's the point?
                    What's gone
stays gone.
                    Trying to preserve it
only shows we're aching to reclaim
  a part of us that vanished
  with it.
            What good are epitaphs?
To dedicate an airport to a President
  means nothing to the airport.
Mountains that we've named for Pike,
  McKinley, or George Everest
  would look the same unnamed.
In one millennium the names
  will fade or change, the photographs
  turn pale, the letters and inscriptions

decompose, and all the etchings
blur and crumble into rubble
like the pyramids.
                    Why not accept
our final legacy as air?
Not air, but breath.
                    Not breath,
but sounds we make from breath.
Not sounds, but words that find
their way from speech to pages
in a book as proof that words
are all that lasts to say
that nothing lasts but words.
Blind Homer sang his poems
seven hundred years
before the birth of Christ.
They sing today in every tongue
on earth plus Braille.
                    And all
those sung or spoken words
were spun from air—just air.

For Those Who Will One Day Live Here

I

Some nights I notice
  teen-age deer determined
  to act like bucks or does.
They roam as if they own
  the place and make it seem
  like I'm the interloper.
                  One shout
  would waken in their wild eyes
  the same dismay I've seen
  in people startled by strangers,
  shock, or death itself.
Tonight the laws of tenancy
  have given them first rights.
I watch them while they graze
  and let them have their fill.

II

Turning from fauna to flora,
  I study how the lilacs
  seem to flow in place.
They prove that beauty in passing
  is only beautiful because
  it's passing.
            Freezing the moment
  like a stopped movie would not
  perpetuate but kill it.
Better to let it pass
  and leave me to my metaphors.
The drooping branches of the wild
  cherry mimic the sadness

of slack flags at half-staff.
A scarf of honeysuckle
 drapes a fence so neatly
 as to make the folderol of cheers
 and hoopla or the pomp of popes
 seem overdone. . . .
                    I watch
 the once and only happen
 only once . . . and only for a time.
But in that time what's meant
 to last like gold keeps burgeoning
 the richer even as it's spent.

Benny Goodman Died While
Playing Mozart on His Clarinet

As endings go, I think
   that Benny Goodman's was consummate.
Dying with the taste of Mozart
   on his lips and breath is difficult
   to top.
               It summarized his life.
More often and dismissively our ends
   choose us with less discrimination,
   but summaries do happen.
                              Harry,
   the neatest of all my colleagues,
   ended seated with his wineglass
   in his hand untipped and not
   a drop spilled.
                     Stricken
   while playing solitaire appeared
   in retrospect correct for Charles
   de Gaulle.
                  And what for one
   unlucky Casanova could have been
   more unexpectedly deserved
   than exiting while hunched and humping
   in the very act?
                     But these
   are all exceptions.
                          Shattered
   by bombs, bullets, crashes,
   crushings, riptides or tornadoes,
   victims by the millions leave us
   little or less to bury.
These are the endings feared
   the most by far too many,

and no one disagrees.
                              But then
we think of Benny Goodman
in his studio alone and playing
something Amadeus wrote
while still a boy.
                              The maestro
played it once, once more
and once again as if to prove
in his finality that practicing the best
made perfect sense—but only
for a time and even then but briefly.

Footnote

The fables of Aesop the slave
  delighted thousands in his time
  and millions since.
                    He wrote
of eagles, serpents, stags
and lions that could talk
two thousand years ahead
of Disney.
             Not only talk
but talk with purpose and always
with a touch of wit . . .
                A peaceful
mouse discovered that kindness
is wasted on the vicious.
                  An ass
that brayed in a lion's skin
was heard by all to be
the ass he was.
             An eagle
was killed by an arrow plumed
with eagle feathers.
             The hare
learned fast but last that speeders
lose to plodders in the end.
Each fable fills a page
  in Aesop's book—one book.
It's been transmitted and translated
  down the centuries with no demise
  in sight.
             To all those scriveners
who brag of title after title
to their names as if profusion
matters more than worth, I cite

one fable frequently forgotten.
Aesop's vixen bore a litter
    twice a year, trumping
    the lioness whose yearly
    whelping was a single cub.
"I have so many babies,"
    boasted the mother-fox,
    "but you have only one."
"Just one," the lioness responded
    while the strutting fox cavorted
    with her brood, " . . . but, a *lion*."

Ballad of a Sniper

This is the way that it happened.
This is the way it was done.
The boy was the son of a hunter,
and his father gave him a gun.

Each day until he was twenty
he slowly perfected his aim.
It was something he did as a hobby,
and his targets were never the same.

War came, and he went to the army.
They noticed how well he could shoot.
They trained him to fly with commandos
and jump with a parachute.

His job was to pick off the leaders
of enemy troops by surprise.
He tracked them like prey in his gunsight,
and the crosshairs were surer than eyes.

By the time he became a civilian
he thought he'd forget what he learned.
He tried to adjust to his family,
but he left, and he never returned.

He went from one job to another
but never could settle on one.
He felt that the world was against him,
and all he could trust was his gun.

He locked himself high in a tower
and targeted people below.

They told him to throw down his weapon.
His answer in bullets was no.

Debating his ultimate choices
of yielding his rifle or not,
he peered down the muzzle and kissed it,
then reached for the trigger and shot.

Choose

*You never know what is enough until you know
what is more than enough.*
—William Blake, "Proverbs of Hell"

When Romans feasted, they opted
  to vomit and then return
  to feast afresh on emptied
  stomachs.
               To us that's gluttony.
To Romans it was dining.
Erotic frescoes near Pompeii
  at Caracalla and Herculaneum offer
  scenes of copulation after copulation.
Morality aside, they illustrate
  how women and men can link
  at the loins while standing, seated,
  supine, prone or otherwise.
We call this fornication.
                              Romans
  called it recreation or relief.
No less a sage than Aristotle
  recognized that man cannot live
  without pleasure.
                     Romans apparently
  agreed.
               But midway between
complete denial and complete
indulgence, Aristotle counseled
moderation.
               Morality again
aside, he settled on the mean
  to balance not enough with overmuch.
Not everyone complies.

Denying every appetite,
   all puritans and stoics cope
   with bodily revolts until
   they die.
            Voluptuaries learn
   that endless pleasure molders
   overnight from boredom into pain.
In search of equilibrium, we place
   our faith in faith, revealed
   or unrevealed.
            With Revelation
   come and gone, we act
   as if it never came.
            Out-moderating
   moderation is our last escape.
We close our minds to mindless
   wars, the poisoning of water
   and the air, a flagging currency
   and vaudevillian politics.
            Only
   the rare immoderates who say
   enough's enough define
   the final options—ridicule
   or blame.
            For better or worse
   it's one or the other, regardless.
Speak up, and be disdained.
Shut up, and be ashamed.

Beginning with Azaleas

Each time I pass azaleas,
  I give them my complete attention.
Not for their colors only—
  although their reds, whites,
  pinks, and lavenders are not
  ignorable—but for their brevity.
A matter of weeks at most . . .
From the first blooms to the last,
  the weeks confirm why Keats
  and Poe believed that beauty
  and sadness existed together.
And I agree.
            To live in full
  for the time given is never
  time enough.
            I feel it
  every time I write.
            The clocks
  stand still for just that long,
  but leaving the written poem
  silent on a page is like
  abandoning a friendship earned
  or watching the azaleas fade.
This makes me balk before the next
  attempt and wonder if it's worth
  the time.
            Why can't I just
  admit I'm not the first
  to cite what Keats and Poe
  believed and leave it go at that?
Others have done so.
            I think
  of Madeline the nun, completely

lucid in her eighties.
                    Younger,
  she had a radiant beauty
  tinged like a nimbus with sadness.
One night by phone we talked
  the years away until
  I asked her shamelessly,
  "Sister, are you still beautiful?"
I heard her smile before
  she said, "Not bad, Sam."
With due respect to Keats
  and Poe, her words said more
  to me than theirs.
                    Or these.

All But the Haunting

The last green gone,
and the brown leaves going . . .
The long nights slow,
and the short days slowing . . .

The head hairs few,
and the temples graying . . .
The facts we deny
are there for the saying.

We learn from the news
that our troubles are massing.
The past is the present,
and the present is passing.

The wounded return
to reunions and kissing.
They're glad to be home,
but their legs are missing.

Where are the brave
who will keep us from killing?
Where is the strength
when the spirit is willing?

If words must be said
for the peace we are seeking,
what is the price
we will pay for not speaking?

The Habits of Perfection

So said Sinatra of his faith,
   "Whatever gets you through the night."
That's quasi-ecumenical,
   but still he had a point.
It seems more sensible than burdening
   each day with absolute denial,
   climbing to a shrine barefooted
   over rocks, repenting in a cell,
   regarding women as subservient
   by nature, lashing the flesh
   with knotted whips or speaking
   not a syllable to anybody
   for a lifetime.
                  Whoever said
that holiness should sentence us
to misery?
            And what of all
those dervishes who twirl until
they topple, penitents who lie
unscreaming over heated
coals, or monks who live
like hermits in the Himalayas?
Extreme examples, to be sure,
   but who can doubt their faith?
I'll take them now and always
   over television's reborn salesmen
   who converse with God out loud,
   harangue the easily converted
   for their tithes, and shout,
   "We stand at Armageddon,
   and we battle for the Lord!"
But even worse are righteous
   murderers like General Pinochet

who "disappeared" his enemies
from helicopters far from shore
by dropping them in handcuffs
in the open sea.
                         Yet Sunday
after Sunday his bishop of choice
would place serenely on his tongue
the body of God in a biscuit.
Earlier by centuries the script
    was similar.
                         Crusaders marched
behind the cross and killed
for Christ.
                         Invaders of the newer
world slew tribes of unbelievers
to extinction.
                         Murder for murder's
sake is reprehensible enough
apart from murdering for God,
but who can say if getting
through the night will let us
wake and be less murderous
by day?
                         Or even sooner?

Deuce

A game long favored by the kings
  of France has made us learn
  its lingo.
              Racquet instead
  of racket—love, derived
  supposedly from *l'oeuf* since eggs
  resembled zeroes, for zero—
  deuce for *dieux* since victory
  from deuce demands two points
  awarded in succession.
                          Although
  no player is ahead at love
  or deuce, a tie at deuce,
  which can repeat itself
  until the match is won,
  offers more drama.
                      Errors
  at love can be redeemed because
  the game is far from over.
A faulty passage early
  in an epic wounds but does not
  kill.
        Errors at deuce
  are unforgiving.
                    A rhyme
  that calls undue attention
  to itself assassinates a poem.
This poem is a case in point.
The most I've done so far
  is serve and volley.
                        As long
  as I can volley, matchpoint

will stay two services
away.
                    Forcing a shot
to win or lose would make
the final score the only
reason for the game.
                              What happens
if I pause right here and let
the poem stay at deuce?
Unfinished symphonies have fared
    as well in music history
    as finished ones.
                              Better
to leave the job uncertain
as a lob at the top of its loft
than risk an ace and miss.
For those to whom finality
    is all that matters, I offer
    the option of permanent deuce.
Stroke by stroke the game
    will just go on and on,
    the clocks will stay irrelevant,
    two players in their prime will prove
    that tennis is the art of poetry
    and prowess in progress, and what
    might seem to some a waste
    of energy and time will last
    forever in the perpetuity of deuce.

The Infinite Sophistication of Human Needs

Instinctively we garb and shield
  our nakedness with clothes.
But no one stops at that.
Color and flare must add
  panache, or else we feel
  no more than nondescript.
No one can deny that water
  ladled from a well would taste
  the same from mugs or Waterford
  crystal.
         But Waterford wins
because it upgrades drinking
into drinking with class.
                We do
the same with everything from fame
to lifetimes.
          Equating fame
with notoriety, we give the infamous
as much attention as the worthy.
Assuming that longevity and true
  fulfillment are synonymous,
we measure life by adding up
  our years.
        I've had enough
of that.
       I favor anything
that's perfect for its purpose
as it is.
      A spoon.
         A baseball.
Lincoln's brevities at Gettysburg.
Why else do I prefer the work
  of those who whittle out of wood

or words what's like no other?
They work from less to little
  to littler to lesser to least.
The carver cuts and sands
  until he bares the clear
  finality of grain.
                  The poet
  writes and pares, re-writes
  and pares again to find what says
  the most with just enough.

Nobody Home

The lawn is putting-green smooth,
   the privets tonsured neatly in a row
   like postulants, the driveway rimmed
   with nightlights and roses.
                            Owned
   in absentia as a fourth address,
   the house is loudly empty.
Twice weekly, a team of maids
   vacuums and dusts.
                      Otherwise,
   the house is so much property—
   real estate.
              The hand-cut wall-stones
   impress me.
              So do the shingles
   from Sicily, the guaranteed "unrustable
   fenestration," the doors and shutters
   of African mahogany.
                  Regardless,
   it all adds up to dark
   and silent dining rooms
   on silent evenings, mornings
   when no one wakes to birdsong,
   and nights as similarly dark
   and still and mute as midnights
   of the deaf and blind.
                Give me
   the clash of laughter over bacon
   breakfasts, coffee and love-talk,
   lightbulbs demanding to be changed,
   and curtains breathing by an open
   window.

Do I exaggerate?
Perhaps.
But passing a locked
villa where nothing matters
more than optimal upkeep
for no one at all offends me.

Lifespans

One puzzler's epitaph could be
  a jigsaw puzzle of Alaska
  left unfinished on a kitchen
  table.
          Another's might be
  purple ballerina slippers
  worn just once.
                  Finality
  makes no allowances.
                      Expected
  or not, it's always a shock.
Without a modicum of tact
  or thoughtfulness, it blunders in
  to silence friendships or affairs
  of state, disrupt religious
  rituals, or sunder lovers
  in the act itself.
                  The more
  it makes no sense, the more
  it makes more sense in retrospect
  than we imagined possible.
Mozart's "Unfinished Symphony"
  profits from being incomplete
  the way assassinated Presidents
  accrue more aura than the spared.
How else can we explain
  why permanence becomes impermanent
  while transience lasts forever?
Who understands the irony of endings?
Whatever happens contradicts
  what we anticipate, and every
  day is like a poem written

line by consequential line
until. . . .

That Far

> *We live by touch.*
>   —Julie Suk

Recorded, their disembodied voices
     sound like music sworn
to silence, but what we hear
are people we loved.
                        We want
     to feel their hands in ours,
     to draw them near, to hold
     them close enough to kiss.
But loving without touch makes love
     the victim of its own desires.
It leaves us seeking difficult
     but possible diversions like trying
     to quote a sonnet by Shakespeare
     in reverse or tying a shoelace
     with one hand or threading
     needles in the dark.
                        Ridiculous?
Of course.
             No matter what
     we do, the dead stay always
     out of touch while we keep
     trying and tying and threading.

To Richard Wilbur in Cummington

Your hymn to the wall-fountain
  at the Villa Sciarra offers me
  the water-music of its splashing
  paradiddles.
            The shrouding snowfall
  in Alsace, Italian laundry
  furling dry from "ruddy gallows,"
  the passage of Fitts and Putnam
  to a "higher standard of living,"
  digging from Jersey to China
  in a dream, observing Mrs. Plath's
  unhappy girl whom love would call
  too late "to the things of this world,"
  muffling the sound of belly
  growls in the presence of the duchess,
  or naming the hilarious debaucheries
  that "bring about the collapse
  of the whole empire"—all these
  are more than verses on a page.
Even those damn ingenious
  riddles you include in all
  your books but which I fail
  to solve are unforgettable. . . .
                Alone
  in Massachusetts now, you spurn
  a life of "private affluence"
  and keep on writing, teaching,
  non-retiring.
           You practice what
  you preached to Ellen once:
  "I wish what I wished you before,
  but harder."

With Charlee gone
but somehow closer in "the other
kingdom," you see "by what
cross-purposes the world is dreamt"
and dance us "back to wonder."
What else should we expect?
Imagination never ages, Dick.
Like God or the present tense
   it is and is and is
   unless corrupted.
               Authors
   of felt speech are fewer
   than ever now among us,
   and fewer still are those
   whose work I call consummate.
But still the world deserves
   a "second finding" in a word
   or words we recognize as true.
That's what a poet does.
That's what your poems do.

To Whom It Will Concern

It bothers me that some day
  you or someone just like you
  will own this house.
                        You'll have
a key—*my* key.
                    You'll paint
  the walls a different color,
  scrap the rugs and change
  my study to a storage room.
Frankly, I feel already
  violated and upset.
                      This place
  is more than property to me.
My wife and I worked hard
  to make it ours.
                    Her tulips,
  lilacs, mums and rhododendrons
  stop whoever's passing by.
I've mown the lawn for years
  and keep it free of weeds.
Our maple tree that shades
  the porch was shorter than a putter
  when we moved here half
  a century ago.
                  What's that
to you?
          You'll cut the maple
  down, re-paint the bedrooms
  prison-gray, let all
  the lilacs die, then stack
  my study high with junk.
Although we've never met
  and never will, I've had

my fill of you.

     Who asked
you here?

     Who gives a tinker's
damn if you'll pay twice
the purchase price or more?
I'll go on saying what I've said
 before.

    I'm staying where I am.
So take your bucks and scram.

Making Do

To shave in arid Catalonia
  in the war, Orwell lathered up
  by mixing soap with Spanish wine.
It made no difference to the razor.
When Grace's zipper separated
  down her spine, she spent all
  evening standing at attention
  in the Shah's pavilion with her back
against a wall.
               That's known
as making do.
               That's what
we do when what needs
doing leaves us little time
and lesser means to do it.
We improvise.
               We seek and settle
for alternatives we never tried
before. . . .
               Because blue paint
was all that was available
in Paris in the war, Picasso
launched what experts call
his "Blue Period."
               That made it
sound intentional.
               Odysseus
suggested that Achilles smuggle
squads of soldiers into Troy
inside a wooden horse.
Achilles smirked and laughed
  but let the scheme unfold
  to show this foolish Ithacan

his dream of making do
was folly.
                    Instead, where armies
failed, deceit prevailed
and won the whole damn war.

One-Liners or Less

What made Elizabeth admit,
  "I'm not attractive to men . . ."
Or Patti state, "My brother
  is so good he's boring."
Or Dolores in her eighties claim,
  "I want more birthdays, but I
  don't want to celebrate them."
Or Barbara, once divorced, concede,
  "The world is ruled by couples."
Such frankness in women makes
  the truth less fearsome
  if admitted when faced,
  and there's a lighter side as well.
Watching his wife in underwear
  peruse the mail, he asked,
  "What if a strange man walked in?"
Without pausing to look up,
  she said, "You are a strange man."
After a party-crasher mocked
  his French hostess by stating,
  "Your meal was fit for a pig,"
  she smiled a Parisian smile
  and said, "So glad you felt
  at home."
          But Marilyn Monroe
outdid them all.
          When asked
if she had something on
when Joe DiMaggio proposed,
she answered with grave innocence,
"The radio. . . ."
          The shorter the line,
the keener the wit—the keener

the wit, the surer the touch—
the surer the touch, the truer
the art that knows when one word
more will be a word too much.

At Large in Provence

I drove due west from Cannes
  like Marco Polo on the loose.
I breathed a chapel's medieval
  oxygen in Thoronet and felt
  I stood exactly in the center
  of the world.
                On Mont Ventoux
I numbered miles and miles
  of France in four directions
  like a king.
             My French was bad
enough to bring unwelcome
  chatter to a welcome halt.
Presences were all that mattered.
From Arles to St. Tropez I passed
  the time deciding only how
  to pass the time.
             In plazas
peopled by strangers I thought
  I'd died and risen as a pilgrim
  of the open road whose goal
  was the horizon.
               Because I fit
the landscape to a tee, I seemed
  much more at home away
  from home than home, and all
  I wanted was to stay
unknown and inconspicuous and free.

Rites

A time comes when life is an order. Just life
without any escapes.
                    —Carlos Drummond de Andrade

All those who loved him came
   in tribute—students, colleagues,
   scholars from out of town,
   two sergeants who gave Regina
   a tucked, tri-folded flag
   after their last salutes.
He would have been embarrassed
   but grateful.
                    Candor he valued
   the most, then fluency, reliability,
   Milton and the Christ of the Beatitudes.
"How much of Milton have you read?"
   he asked a doctoral candidate.
"Not much," she said, "I'm still
   in structuralism."
                    Faced with that,
   the skills he'd mastered to interrogate
   the most recalcitrant Vietcong
   were useless.
                    Exactitude defined him
   when he proved that Shakespeare's
   active vocabulary exceeded
   Churchill's by tens of thousands
   or saw all military vanity
   exposed in Milton's—"He
   who overcomes by force
   hath overcome but half his foe."
If staying rational when riled
   or being moral in immoral

times defined a man
of consequence, he was that man.
Nothing could make him curse,
  including the final sickness
  he regarded as a challenge.
                              But valor
did nothing but delay the chapel
rituals.
          The closed coffin
numbed us like a door slammed shut.
It let us leave to live
  the lives we left . . .
                    But better.

          For Albert Labriola

PART SEVEN
Bare-Wristed

Have a Nice Day

I shovel up what's left
  of a wild rabbit smattered
  on the road.
              It leaves a red
memento of itself . . . .
                   Years back,
  my neighbor would be mowing,
  pruning or watering his roses.
Now he neither speaks nor walks
  and cannot recognize the woman
  shaving him or changing his pajamas
  as his wife.
             Later, while swallowing
coffee and headlines, I skim
  this morning's harvest from the killing
  fields surnamed the world.
Inch by column inch,
  a list of military losses
  lengthens like a final bookmark
  or a grim receipt.
               Nasdaq
and the Dow show gains although
  the news today is worse
  than yesterday's.
             One analyst
alliterates that "greed is not
  accountable to grief or glee."
Crossword puzzles, sports,
  the comics and the elegiac prose
  of the obituaries serve as filler.
It's cloudy in New York, sunny
  in Detroit and sweltering in Santa Fe.

Scattered "shower activity"
  is predicted locally by midnight.
My neighbor, mute and unremembering,
  is spared all this.
                      For him
  it's yesterday forever.
                      Am I
  the wiser if I strive to know
  what's going on?
                   Or is it all
  a waste of time since history's
  "the propaganda of the victor" anyway?
I fold the paper like a used
  tissue, its news passé.
Nothing's the way it seems.
Tomorrow's headlines will erase
  today's as surely as the rabbit stain
  by morning will be rained away.

The Imperfectionist

I've come to debase the currency.
—Diogenes

You want a perfect world,
   but that's a dreamer's currency.
I see a world no worse
   or better than the world in fact.
What I pronounce unchangeable
   you plan to change.
                    Don't be
a fool.
            Societies flourish
only when they face and deal
with imperfections you're determined
to eliminate.
                    Let's start with crime.
Abolish crime, and you
   abolish lawyers, judges,
   uniformed police, detectives,
   bail bondsmen, prisons
   and *habeas corpus.*
                    Then think
of what you lose without disease.
Physicians, nurses, surgeons,
   lab technicians, health plans,
   pharmacists, to name a few....
Lately you've even talked
   of ending war.
                    That means
no more marines, sailors,
soldiers, bunker-busting
bombers, drones and clusters
in reserve, and all the industries

of ordnance that offer jobs
to millions.
             Think of the losses.
My view for what it's worth
  would be to let perfectionism
  die because it's unattainable.
Such currency's been long debased
  by what's imperfect now
  and always.
            It makes us see
that we must earn our lives
by learning how to compensate
for our deficiencies.
            That's never
going to change.
           You'd think
that poetry would be exempt,
but you'd be wrong.
          Compared
to silence, which can say without
a word what nothing else can say,
all poets are deficient.
           No matter
how they're moved to say
what never can be said,
silence says it better.

Dressing Down

Women deal with panties, hooks
  and straps while men have only
  tops and trunks between
  their haberdashery and skin.
Not underwear as much as
  innerwear, they make accessible
  to women comfort and support,
  to men convenience.
                 Double-slung,
  the breasts repose.
            Below
  the waistbands of their briefs
  men cup their privates in a netting
  pouch that vents a peephole.
Intermingled randomly as laundry,
  these inners turn into themselves
  again, immaculately stacked
  to do what they were made to do.
If I see poetry in underwear—
  or rather, innerwear—who says
  I'm wrong?
           There's not a thing
  superfluous, no ornamental
  fluff and nothing else but what
  relates to function.
             Anyone
  in innerwear seems primed
  for the next step to outerwear
  or the last stop en route
  to love or sleep or a shower.
That's how the living live.
Compare all this to sculptures
  of the gods and goddesses of Greece

and Rome in poses of voluptuous
perfection.
        With nothing to pull off
or on, they seem to me
just bare at best.
        And sad.

From the Feet Up

Suppose you dropped a microwave
   on your right foot's bare toes.
I did.
        It broke all five.
Predictably they healed askew.
Since then I've had to wear
   a larger shoe by half
   a size with a wider toe-box.
It's given me a hitherto
   unknown respect for feet.
The runner I used to be
   is gone for good.
                The dancer
   I presumed I was is not
   a step less wooden.
                        After
   a hard hike I walk
   flat-footed for a week.
Last night I studied my foot
   the way cartographers survey
   a map they've drawn apparently
   from space.
                The bones and tendons
   slanted snugly underskin.
The veins spread faintly blue
   until they deepened.
                        Everything
   was primed to keep upright
   the rest of me.
                But how?
I asked a doctor to explain
   what keeps us from collapsing

in apparent disregard of gravity
each time we stand.
                    "I don't
know how," he sighed, "except
to say what keeps us up
is *life—just life.*"
                    I said
that sounded hardly scientific.
"The dead can't stand," he said
with medical certainty as if
that fact alone confirmed
his previous assumption.
                    And it did.

At My Age

Some think I should be vaguely
    grateful or embarrassed or both.
"At your age," they warn, "you must
    be careful."
                    Careful of what?
I'm watchful when I walk or drive,
    but who can foil lightning,
    break a fall or keep
    the brakes from failing on a hill?
Frankly, I'm past the age
    of caring.
                    Outliving those
    I love is what I fear
    much more than any fate
    avoidable by care.
                            The work
    that dares me most is what
    I make with words, and that's
    as difficult as ever.
                            Otherwise
    I tend to family needs
    as needed, answer letters
    with a fountain pen and hope
    a poem-to-be will come my way.
Since poetry like love can never
    be coerced or rushed, I've learned
    to wait.
                    If something happens,
    I cooperate.
                    If not, I read.
Reading for me is conversation
    at its best.

Conversing, page
by page, with Shakespeare, Galeano,
Hemingway, Camus or Rilke
assures me that the wine of words
improves with age.
                    It's quite
miraculous when something written
centuries or decades back
seems just as present as today.
Such work rewards the workman
  with a second life that's truer
  than the one he lived.
                    That's why
I read what age can never age
until I'm ready to cooperate
with what intrudes like love
and chooses me to have its say.

Bare-Wristed

After I broke my watch,
   I ate only when hungry,
   slept when I was tired,
   woke when I had slept
   enough and never thought—
   not once—of death.
                        Uncuffed
   at the wrist from punctuality
   I lived scot free in space
   with no concern for A.M.
   or P.M.
                  Daybreak was sun,
   and night was darkness and the moon.
Arriving anywhere on schedule
   mattered less than just meandering
   along the way.
                     That made
   the going more adventurous
   than getting there.
                        Perhaps
   that's why I never wore
   my watch to bed.
                        Since sleep
   and dreams seemed infinite as space,
   what place was left for time?
After I had my watch
   repaired, I found myself
   re-sentenced to the world of prose
   where hours, months and years
   demanded to be counted.
                              I saw
   no poetry in that and turned

instead to open-ended space
that mocked the clocks and offered
everything at large to anyone
who took the time to look.

And the Winner Isn't

She stands alone with arms
  (if she had arms) akimbo.
Without a head, she lets us
  dream she's smiling, frowning,
  ready to speak or just
  plain bored.
           The absence of legs
  suggests a woman totally
  at ease without a stitch.
The breasts, if you must know,
  are not in textbook lingo
  "pendant when mature."
             Upright
  in stone they seem too rounded
  for descent.
        Ditto the hips
  that shape a delta to the cleft
  where stone and statue stop.
Whoever carved and polished
  smooth this headless Venus
  did it, I am told, by hand.
Without electric tools he worked
  like Michelangelo with nothing else
  but mallets, chisels, and the skill
  to ransom elegance from stone.
Even without a head and four
  appendages, what's left bespeaks
  entirety amid the junk.
I tour a gallery of Warhol
  wannabes, pseudo-Pollocks
  and other surfacers and splashers.
Their lure is lost on me—
  as is the floor-to-ceiling

canvas chosen "Best
in Show."

        Totally covering
one wall, it's painted uniformly
gray.

        It's titled "Gray."

Flyover

Romping across my lawn,
  a pair of teenage deer
  outprance each other to the street.
After they've trotted off,
  the lawn invites me to enjoy
  its weedlessness.
               The calla lilies
  aim their yellow bugles
  at the sun.
           Azaleas, irises
  and tulips flaunt their blooms
  in every color but black.
A robin, three sparrows and a wren
  compete in birdsong with the caw
  and cackle of a single crow.
Why is it then that batteries
  in both my hearing aids
  announce they're shutting down?
Or someone I have never met
  will phone me, ask if I'm Sam
  and urge me to prevent extinction
  of the apes in Zanzibar?
                Or trios
  of fighter jets in arrowhead
  formations, wing to wing,
  will thunder overhead and spoil
  the perfect silence of the sky.

Downing a Maple

Spike-booted and safety-belted
  up the slimming trunk, he aims
  his clipper at the topmost limbs
  and clips.
            The highest branches
spiral down like sorrows in leaf.
Those that are thicker plummet
  and gouge the lawn.
              He clips
and saws until the trunk
is all that's left.
          Scarred
by amputation like a mast
without a sail, it's ready
to be sectioned, chunked and trucked
away for kindling.
            De-stumping's
next, and that means grinding
down and grinding down
the butt to sawdust.
          Fifty
summers saw it grow
from man-high to house-high
to double-house-high.
           It shaded
the porch so he could read.
It never cracked through half
  a century of storms and ice.
But when its roots attacked
  the water-pipes, it had to go.
Tonight he'll bury scraps
  of branch and bark inside
  the hole it left.

He'll top
the grave with sod and mulch
and seed it with rye.
In a month
no one will know the difference.

Meryl Streep, Actress

By living a life that's not
   her own but somehow more
   her own than possible, she goes
   beyond the script.
                     It's more
than training, make-up or photography.
It's even more than talent.
Her accents—British, Polish,
   Danish or Italian—are surer
   in their perfect imperfection
   than exact facsimiles.
                  Rowing
upriver, crossing a covered
bridge, inviting dalliance
on a train or being a Prime
Minister, novelist or nun
are more than roles for her.
They seem like ventures cautiously
   begun and ending better
   than expected.
               Some say
   it's just an exercise in craft.
To me that totally ignores
   the mystery.
             More so by genius
than direction, the way she acts
defines performance as an art
and not a trade.
             It's death
and resurrection all at once.
That's why I praise this lady
   with the same care I take
   to save this poem from excess.

Seeing her consummately composed
  in every part she plays,
  I never feel betrayed.

Happenstance

It could be trivial as finding
   lost keys or a missing sock.
Or monumental as discovering
   a use for penicillin purely
   by accident.
           Or life-altering
as genuine love that's finally
unplanned but irrefuseable.
The past's replete with incidents
   that prove how chance much more
   than choice creates what we
   regale as history.
           Heading
   for Cathay, Columbus blundered
   into islands south of Florida.
He never sailed to North
   America, regardless of the myth.
But still he gets the credit.
Pope Clement VIII relished
   an Arab Muslim dinner
   drink distilled from arabicas.
He even blessed it.
           Coffee
   so grandly Christianized filled
   cups thereafter by the billions
   throughout Europe and the West....
Yesterday, while driving and striving
   "to think globally and act
   locally" about the rising cost
   of fuel, planetary warming,
   urban crime, the possibilities
   of war and other urgencies,

I listened to Ravel's "Bolero"
on the stereo.
                    I stopped at a light
beside an SUV driven
by a white-haired man in a beret.
The light turned green.
                         He smiled,
raised his hand and said
what looked like "Wait."
                         I waited.
Ravel's "Bolero" overwhelmed
   the siren of a speeding ambulance
   that passed in front of us.
It would have crushed me
   had I gone ahead.
                    The man
in the beret was thinking locally
of nothing else at just
that moment.
                    He looked relieved
and, having merely saved my life,
just turned and drove away.

To Be in Byblos

To drive beside the sea
to Byblos from Beirut
and back is bound
to broaden your belief
in matters biblical.
Born and brought
from Byblos, the Bible
branded its believers
as the People of the Book.
Boarding a boat
in Byblos, Paul
of Tarsus brought
the blessings of beatitude
to breeds below
and far beyond the Bosporus.
The ballads of Adonis
were begun and sung
in Byblos, and his wounds
are now anemones that blossom
where his river bleeds
and broadens in the bay.
Because of Byblos
we are beckoned to believe
that birth and death—
which bookend both our
being here and having been—
are not the be-
and-end-all of the free,
brief bounty of our breath.

In Due Course

The traveler I used to be
　　is bored with destinations now.
To drive or fly to where
　　I've been before can never be
　　the same, so why bother?
In conversations I repeat
　　some lines I've said already
　　more than once, but not
　　as well.
　　　　　　And so I wonder
　　if I'm losing touch—in whole
　　or part.
　　　　　　It leaves me stalled
　　like those whose fear of death
　　makes them forget to live,
　　which means they're dead already.
That's just not right.
　　　　　　　　What's worse
　　is living on like men who've lost
　　their wives and say the present's
　　not the future they imagined
　　in the past.
　　　　　　That's understandable
　　for widowers but otherwise a waste
　　of time.
　　　　　　But let's be frank.
From birth we live a breath
　　away from requiems and God.
Each day the challenge stays the same.
What's now is up to us.
What's next is not.
　　　　　　Preparing
　　for the unpredictable or wishing

to be stilled while sleeping to avoid
the throes or boasting of our years
as if the one who lives
the longest wins does nothing
but depress.
                    Who prophesied that age
should make us glum?
                              There's still
the miracle of freshly baked
baguettes, evenings with those
we love, the Grierson texts
of John Donne's poetry,
a blank notebook and a pen,
a pipe with my preferred tobacco,
and the rare but possible bounty
of an exit while at home and busy.

To Adam

Your poems breathe.
                     The words
are never in a hurry, never
forced into coherence, never
inexact.
               You let your subjects
choose themselves and speak
through you, but still the voice
is yours—just yours.
                    For me
that's everything.
                 If poetry's
no more than playing with words
and not real conversation at its best,
why deal with it?
               Your poems
have the sacredness of secrets
shared with proven friends.
Your essays do the same.
You write of Rilke as a fellow
craftsman, never as Goethe's
sacrosanct, untouchable successor.
Milosz and Szymborska you praise
as more than fellow Poles—
Milosz, for persevering to the end—
Szymborska, for poems that match
her candor in declining speaking
junkets in her eighties thus,
"Madam Szymborska will come
when she is younger."
                 All this
reveals a total generosity
that's rare in general, rarer

in writers and rarest in poets.
Whoever said that living well
   requires maximum detachment
   plus maximum appreciation?
For you that comes as naturally
   as speaking Polish or gazing
   at your wife's face or strolling
   down a street near Montparnasse.
In Houston, Krakow or Paris
   you grant what's suddenly
   important just because it's *there*
   the courtesy of absolute attention.
Like Romeo embracing Juliet.
Like doctors in surgery.

               Like Angelo
Roncalli, the plump, old pope,
who spoke the same to Kennedy
and Krushchev as to countrymen
from Bergamo, the Vatican guards
and the organ-grinder smiling
with his monkey near the Piazza Navona.

Joe Louis's Daughter

For years before he met
  and married Candace, George's
  forté was Louis lore.
We listened to a time re-lived:
  Candace, smiling and relaxed;
  George, regaling us with fistiana.
"Conn tried to slug with Louis,
  and it cost him the fight,
  and Billy heard it from Joe
  himself when he visited him
  at the end, 'You had the title
  for twelve rounds before
  you lost it.'"
              He spoke
of Louis's time in the army,
" . . . ninety-six exhibition bouts,
  and he refused to box at all
  before a segregated audience."
She smiled a daughter's smile
  and nodded.
             Finally we talked
of Schmeling, Mauriello, Walcott,
Baer and Marciano.
               "Rocky
was in tears after he knocked
Joe out of the ring."
            Then came
the down years of refereeing,
wrestling and working as a greeter
in Las Vegas.
         "Open-heart
surgery stopped him," she said
and paused, remembering.

"Sinatra
picked up the bill for that,"
he said.
            "And don't forget
the funeral, George," she added,
"Uncle Francis paid for everything."

Flair

I'm sick of seasons.
                    What once
  was green is heaped for burning
  now or raked aside for three
  cold months to molder into mulch.
Like everyone I'm sentenced to wait
  for April's answer to November.
Some say life moves in cycles.
I call that boring.
                Give me
  what contradicts the clocks and stays
  itself despite appearances.
Was Troy so different from a tree
  gone bare?
              Who cares if top
  geographers have shown precisely
  where it was and when?
                   It took
  a poet to reveal what doomed it
  to extinction—a war for ports
  of call decided by deception
  and stubbornly prolonged to save
  the honor of a jilted Greek.
Melodramatic as that sounds,
  it resonates with fiscal and domestic
  issues found in all wars since.
There's nothing seasonal about it.
What something or someone was
  or said or did survives
  not resurrected but repeated
  like a variation on a single theme.
I find it true in cosmic,
  cosmopolitan or common matters.

Mary Stockhausen loved berets
and wore them at a tilt
in formal or informal gatherings.
They conjured what the French call flair.
At Mary's funeral her children
wore berets in Mary's honor
tilted in the selfsame way.

Womankind

Begin with childbirth.
                    Though men
  beget what women bear,
  no one denies that bearing
  is the harder job.
                    Medea
  silenced all of Jason's military
  bombast with six words, "You
  could not face childbirth
  once."
                    Onward to nurturing . . . .
However tasteful their providers,
  women have a way of making
  anything provided better.
And what of rearing and protecting
  the young . . . .
                    Seeing their offspring
  threatened or harmed, mothers
  can be roused to rage the way
  a lioness with cubs at risk
  can be more lethal than a lion.
As for concern?
                    Women are known
  to care for loved ones
  to the end, and afterward revere
  their memories with even more
  devotion.
                    What else?
                    Less often
  with women than with men, the dice
  of dalliance will find excuses
  to be cast.
                    What more?

                                    In sculpture,
          painting or photography the female
          figure nude appears
          in unadorned indifference.
                                    Speaking
          of figures, the female body
          is described by some as floral
          in its very architecture, graceful
          in motion or at ease but still
          with all its mysteries concealed.
That makes for undeniable attraction,
          and women undeniably attract.
Why else did Victor Hugo write,
          "A woman naked is a woman
          armed."
                                    Is that deniable?

April Fool

My friend was found to have
  a tumor.
               Yesterday, surgery.
Today, a promising prognosis.
A week ago—nothing.
Then suddenly surprise and shock
  and finally, thank God, relief.
Who relishes bad news
  befalling friends?
               But why
surprise and shock?
               I've known
for decades how the unexpected rules
our lives for good or ill
despite our hoping otherwise.
Confronting this absurdity,
  I've learned that wisdom matters
  little, and virtue even less
  in making sense of such intrusions.
Intrusions?
          What if they're not?
What if the folly of our dreams
  and wishful planning or the utter
  vanity of thinking what
  will be will be are truly
  the intrusions?
            Or if our thoughts
  and acts are mere reprieves—
  like dalliances indulged by dilettantes—
  before the unavoidable and likely?
I've said these things before.
They leave me trapped between
  conviction and confusion.

                    Meanwhile,
    the world remains the world
    where pink and white umbrellas
    of the Japanese cherry flourish
    in furious bloom.
                    The squawks
    of jays and robins overwhelm
    the tweets of lesser fry.
And daily after school my neighbor's
    daughter with Down's Syndrome
    plays on her backyard swing.
All afternoon she knows the bliss
    that only the unknowing know
    and swings and swings and swings.

Don't Just Do Something, Stand There

As much as we prefer the orderly,
  it's only the disordered or disorderly
  that stays in mind and makes us
  choose to act.
              Imperfect
from the start we know perfection's
out of reach but not perfectibility,
and so we try to rectify
what's flawed.
         We fix.
               We learn
to compensate.
         We cope.
              We foster
arts and sciences to remedy our
failings: learning versus ignorance—
justice over malice—medicine
and care against disease.
Of course, some choose renunciation
  to avoid the challenge.
             They might
create their exit with a gun—
or call irrelevant the sustenance
of music, poetry and art—
or think the Second Coming's
answer to our wishful dreams
is always imminent.
           But what's
the point?
        The world is not
that easily renounced.
            Right now
it's all we have.

                    Nothing
will make our inconvenient dyings
more depressing than regretting what
we should have done or could
have paused to do....
                            For half
an hour yesterday my wife
sat smiling and alone to view
an orchid in full bloom.
                            Her smile
and the orchid said whatever's
beautiful beyond belief
is even moreso, being brief.

Ace

At sixteen his part-time job
  is watching the tennis court
  to free the pro for lunch.
With no one to play against
  he shows no interest in the game
  until I challenge him.
                    Smiling,
  he turns tiger on the court.
His forehand, slam, and backhand
  make his base-line lobs
  or drop-shots at the net
  unhittable.
                    Each ball I serve
  or stroke comes back at twice
  the speed.
                    I lose two sets
  at love . . . .
                    He shakes my hand
  to help me feel less helpless
  than I feel.
                    Relaxed, he turns
  into his job again.
                    The change
  from prowess to repose reminds me
  how the best of actors, dancers,
  poets and chefs resume
  their lives between performances.
They look relaxed and totally
  indifferent to their own perfection.

The Poetry of Laughing, Yawning and Singing

Whatever I found so funny
  I've forgotten, but I laughed.
And laughed.
          I laughed myself
  simple.
       Nobody else
was laughing, but a few smiled
to see me laugh, then laughed
themselves.
         Soon everyone
was laughing just because
I laughed....
         Some use the word
"infectious" to explain this type
of rippling effect.
           That's much
  too medical for me.
           Why not
admit it's more akin to why
we yawn when someone near us
starts to yawn?
        Or how
a song keeps singing in us
even when the song is done?
Later we sing or hum it
to ourselves, which means it's never
really over.
        That's why
the way we live with comedy,
fatigue, and music leads me
straight to poetry.
         I'm stunned
sullen by those who say

that poetry is nothing more
than wordplay, syntax,
sociology and scholarship.
I say a poem happens
randomly as laughter, yawns
or songs, but how or when
is always unexplainable and sudden.

Exits

What pens once meant to writers,
  needles meant to her.
                    Anchoring
  buttons was her equivalent
  of finding the right words
  and sewing them in place
  on cuffs, collars and sleeves.
Zippers she scorned.
                    Buttons
  held things together as she did
  by living for others, and of
  all others we came first.
When seamstressing her dresses,
  she said that dressing up
  (but tastefully) was every woman's
  poetry.
              Dying while getting dressed
  became for her, in retrospect,
  the best exit.
              That took me
  decades to accept.
                    But then
  what's better than leaving
  in full stride?
              Confirming this
  by contrast was a letter I received
  this morning from the best of friends.
"Pray for my wife," he wrote
  in closing, "the Alzheimer's worsens."

The Driven Driver

Lured by the "passionate pursuit
    of perfection," I bought a Lexus.
Motor Trend proclaimed my car
    reliable but "boring."
                        Outranked
    by Jaguar XK ("sex
    on wheels"), Cadillac STS
    ("matching the Germans"), Aston
    Martin D89 ("guaranteed
    front row valet parking"),
    Mercedes CLS ("sensuality
    trumps sensibility"), and Lamborghini
    Gallardo ("breathtaking"), I felt
    outclassed.
                And yet as one
    who craves creative boredom,
    I prefer my car without
    "trim tweaks."
                    The CD player
    relieves the quiet boredom
    of long trips.
                    The mauve
    seat leather boringly offsets
    the black obsidian exterior.
I'm soothed by the boring motor,
    and a cruising button lets me
    steer toward horizons with both
    feet bored and unemployed.
I guess a Bentley might be
    more exciting, but excitement
    often changes to regret the way
    that something long desired loses
    its attraction when possessed.

So I ignore "breathtaking sensuality
   that matches the Germans for front row
   valet parking."
                My car
  is car enough for me.
Unless I'm wrong, what else
  is traveling but sitting still
  while being sped from where
  I am to some place else
  intact, on time and reliably bored?

Inconveniently Themselves

I recognize all five of them—
  a doe, three fauns and a teen-age
  stag whose antlers-to-be
  are still just knobs.
             They'd traipsed
  across my yard all summer,
  nosing for apples or nipping
  my wife's azaleas.
            I'd scare
  them off, but once I said,
  "Just wait a minute!"
            I rolled
  a fallen apple to the doe.
She paused to size me up,
  then tongued the apple, bit,
  chomped and left some remnants
  for the fauns.
            The stag preferred
  his personal apple and ate it
  whole . . .
            Now, in absolute
  indifference to stalled traffic,
  they cross a four-lane road
  in single file at a stoplight.
They take their time.
            Finally,
  one driver fires a staccato
  honk and makes them halt.
The doe appears less startled
  than offended.
            She stares at half
  a block of drivers furious

and anxious to be anywhere
but where they are.

                        Her stance
reminds them of a past when deer
could roam and rollick here
before there was a road,
before the world was ruled
by stoplights, clocks and cars,
before what everyone calls
everything existed . . . .

                        Of course,
the traffic wins at last
but not before five deer,
ancestral as gazelles and queued
like players in a play within a play,
have paused and posed and passed.

Ultimatum

What difference does it make
    if Robert Frost had
    afterthoughts about the road
    not taken?
                Or why the life
    we lose in living speaks
    to us in all of Thornton
    Wilder's plays?
                Perhaps
    it comes from second-guessing
    choices that we make.
                        But why?
If what we choose to be
    results in who we are,
    why resurrect alternatives
    or see rejected options
    as regrets?
                Whatever could
    have qualified as possibilities
    has long since vanished.
                            Why
    wage a rearguard war
    with might have, should have,
    could have?
                But still we do,
    regardless.
                Nothing's absolute
    until we see that everybody's
    next day and last day will be
    the same day some day.
                            No
    options there—not one.

Near Enough

Occasional deer, wild turkeys,
   rabbits or high winds will light
   a bulb I've mounted in the yard
   to startle flowerbed intruders.
Any sound or presence will ignite
   what's always itching to illuminate.
Often at midnight it glows
   and tints my neighbor's yard
   and half of mine with noon.
Nearness turns it on—just nearness.
Tonight it makes me think
   of patients surfacing from comas
   after they hear the voice
   of one they love.
                Or lifelong
   mates who have identical
   thoughts while working side
   by side in silence.
                Or those
   held dear but long since gone
   becoming dearer being gone.
It all comes down to nearness.
At first, nothing.
            Then, light.
Then, love.
         Otherwise, the darkness.

Definitely

Birthdays keep me changing
  day by day into my final self—
but simplified.
          No longer
occupied with titles, job
descriptions, honors, meetings
to attend, awards or trips
abroad, I'm back to who
I am.
        I answer to my name
with or without the Mister.
Nothing's unimportant now.
When faraway friends or former
  students write me, I return
  the courtesy by thanking them
by pen.
        Knowing my wife's
in pain, depressed, or wronged
lets nothing matter more
until she smiles.
                Love makes
whatever's threatening or risky
unignorable because finality
is always possible.
                That leaves me
thoughtfully mortal.
                For those
who have such thoughts, the fear
of loss exceeds the fear
of death itself.
                Boasters
who say their love's the sum

of numbered anniversaries have much
to learn.
                    For me it's one
long, short day when sudden
jeopardies are lived with or through.
If we survive, we're thankful
  we were spared the worst.
                              Later
  we seek assurance in religion
  and philosophy but find no more
  than ritual and contradiction.
As for the arts?
                    Even
  the finest fail to go where
  art returns us to ourselves.
Since novelty outsells perfection,
  painters seem content to stipple,
  splash and spray.
                         Poems
  appear as trick typography
  or messages from pen-pals
  to pen-pals or surface sociology
  without imagination.
                          Dancing
  is aerobics with an attitude . . . .
Finding little that redeems,
  I live a life without
  adornment with my chosen one
  whose daily presence is a gift,
  a son, a daughter-in-law-
  and-love and three grandchildren
  growing up into themselves
  so quickly that I'm always
  in arrears on birthday counts.

The children smile and correct me.
I stand corrected.
                And grateful.